ORIGAMI BOXES

ORIGAMI BOXES

MARK BOLITHO

jacqui small

First published in 2018 by
Jacqui Small
an imprint of The Quarto Publishing Group
The Old Brewery
6 Blundell Street
London N7 9BH, United Kingdom
T (0)20 7700 6700 F (0)20 7700 8066
www.QuartoKnows.com

Publisher: Jacqui Small
Commissioning and Project Editor: Joanna Copestick
Managing Editor: Emma Heyworth-Dunn
Senior Designer and Art Director: Rachel Cross
Designer: Clare Thorpe
Production: Maeve Healy

ISBN: 978 1 911127 13 0

A catalogue record for this book is available
from the British Library.

2020 2019 2018
10 9 8 7 6 5 4 3 2 1

Printed in China

Scaling and Sizes

Each project is accompanied by a scaling diagram that shows the size of the final model compared to the starting sheet of paper. The diagram is based on a square sheet with dimensions of 18 x 18cm (7 x 7in), or an equivalent rectangle. However, larger or smaller models can be made. The size of the final model can be scaled up or down by comparing the dimensions of the paper used to the sheet used in the scaling diagram.

Complexity Ratings

The projects in this book have been given a rating based on their complexity. They appear beneath the title of each project.

Easy ✳

Intermediate ✳✳

More Challenging ✳✳✳

CONTENTS

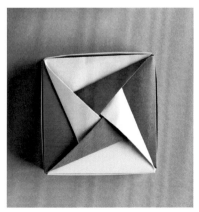
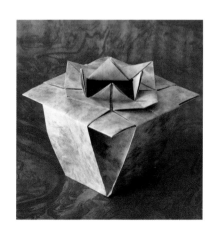

MINDFUL ORIGAMI

Welcome to the world of origami, the art of paper folding. At its heart it is turning a sheet of paper into a finished model. However, it's not only a matter of creating the final result, but also a journey of paper transformation that involves creativity and contemplation along the way to produce your finished piece of work.

The word 'origami' comes from the Japanese word for paper folding. In the East the craft developed based on standard forms and traditional designs and it now has many enthusiasts around the world.

The Internet has enabled the sharing of ideas and lead to a collective enthusiasm for developing more beautiful and complex designs. In the chase for complexity, however, some of the beauty of the craft has been overlooked. This is an oversight I hope to overcome with this book, by presenting mindful finished works in appropriate colours and compositions.

The paper-folding process can be a contemplative journey, over time a plain sheet of paper is transformed into something wonderful. The satisfaction of origami comes not only from creating interesting designs, but also from following the folding journey and seeing your model evolve at your fingertips. Origami offers a perfect way to explore your mindful creativity in the colours and paper choices you use.

The models in this collection have been selected based on the aesthetic quality of the final model and the folding processes. They are explained with step-by-step diagrams that show the sequence of folds needed to produce the final design.

At the start of the collection I have included instructions for an Easy Box (see page 10). This is an opportunity to gain familiarity with the diagrams and symbols used to explain the folding sequence. Some models are more complex than others and we have given a rating to each project as a guide (see page 4). If you are new to origami, try starting with the easier models and working up to the more complex projects.

I hope you enjoy folding these projects as much as I enjoyed selecting them.

GETTING STARTED

Here are the basic folding techniques and symbols you'll need to complete the projects in the book.

FOLDING IN HALF

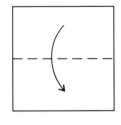

1. The step indicates that the paper should be folded in half.

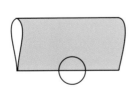

2. First of all line up the opposite sides of the paper and hold the edges together.

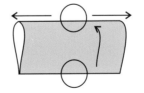

3. When the two layers are aligned, pinch the middle to hold them together. Then make the crease.

4. The paper is accurately folded in half.

ARROWS AND FOLDS

Paper folding instructions explain the folding process with a series of steps leading to a finished model. Each step explains one or two folds in the process. Steps should be followed in order and when a step is completed, it should resemble the image shown in the next step.

The transition from one step to the next is shown by a series of lines and arrows indicating where folds should be made. The lines show where to fold and the arrows show how the paper should be moved to make folds.

Folds are described as either Mountain Folds or Valley Folds.

These folds refer to how the surface will look after the fold has been completed. A Mountain Fold will fold towards the observer, forming a mountain shape, while the Valley Fold will fold away, forming a V or valley shape. They are represented by different dotted-line symbols.

ARROWS

- Fold
- Fold and unfold
- (2) Fold over 2 layers

FOLDS

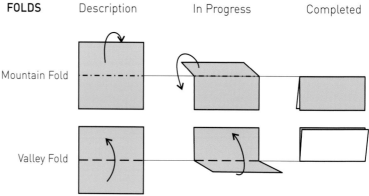

	Description	In Progress	Completed
Mountain Fold			
Valley Fold			

ORIGAMI SYMBOLS

Various symbols are used to explain the folding process, such as turning the model over, rotating the model, or repeating a step. The symbols on the right are the ones used in this book.

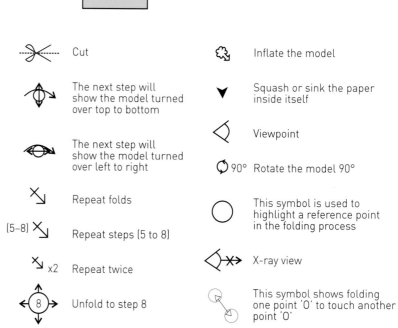

- Cut
- The next step will show the model turned over top to bottom
- The next step will show the model turned over left to right
- Repeat folds
- (5–8) Repeat steps (5 to 8)
- x2 Repeat twice
- 8 Unfold to step 8
- Inflate the model
- Squash or sink the paper inside itself
- Viewpoint
- 90° Rotate the model 90°
- This symbol is used to highlight a reference point in the folding process
- X-ray view
- This symbol shows folding one point 'O' to touch another point 'O'

DIAGRAMS

The diagrams are shown in two colours, with the coloured side being the front and the white side being the reverse. This should make the step-by-step instructions easier to follow.

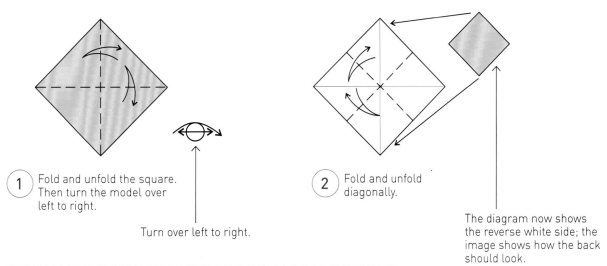

1 Fold and unfold the square. Then turn the model over left to right.

Turn over left to right.

2 Fold and unfold diagonally.

The diagram now shows the reverse white side; the image shows how the back should look.

THE FOLLOWING IS A LONGER SEQUENCE TO MAKE A PRELIMINARY BASE.

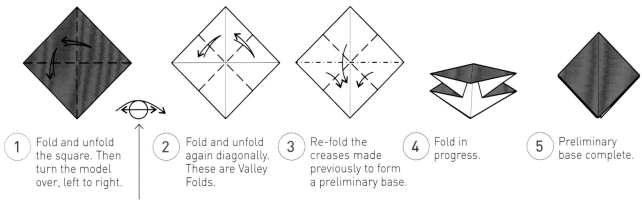

1 Fold and unfold the square. Then turn the model over, left to right.

Turn the model over.

2 Fold and unfold again diagonally. These are Valley Folds.

3 Re-fold the creases made previously to form a preliminary base.

4 Fold in progress.

5 Preliminary base complete.

Origami instructions take you through a step-by-step process from start to finish. Symbols are included to explain the transition from one step to the next (see opposite). Each step shows how the folded project should look and shows the folds that should be applied to progress to the next step.

When approaching a step, look ahead to the next diagram to see how the model should look when the fold has been applied. Then check that the paper model you are making resembles the step diagram. Look out for reference points to compare your model with the instructions to make sure you remain on the right track. If your model doesn't resemble the step you are on, unfold the last step and work back until it does.

Easy Box

*

This box works by folding the edges of a square inand beneath one another to form a flat model that then opens out to become a box shape.

18 X 18CM (7 X 7IN)

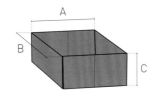

A 6cm   (2⅓in)
B 6cm   (2⅓in)
C 3cm   (1¼in)

START WITH A SQUARE, COLOURED SIDE UP.

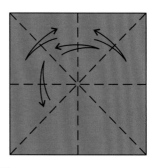

1 Fold and unfold the square in half lengthwise and diagonally through the middle of the paper.

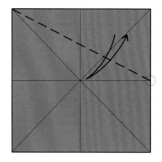

2 Fold and unfold between the upper corner and where the middle crease touches the opposite side.

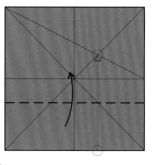

3 Fold the lower edge up to touch the intersection of the creases. This marks a third of the square.

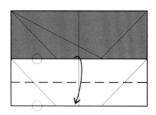

4 Fold the edge back down to touch the lower folded edge.

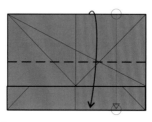

5 Fold the upper edge down to the lower edge.

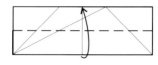

6 Fold the upper layer up to the folded edge above.

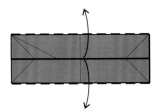

7. Fold the folded sections out as shown. This will leave the edges of the square folded up behind.

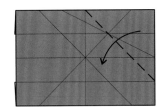

8. Fold one corner in. The upper edge should touch the middle crease of the paper.

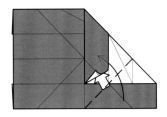

9. Fold the lower corner up and into the upper section (indicated by the arrow). The lower edge should touch the middle crease.

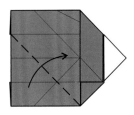

10. Fold the opposite lower corner up.

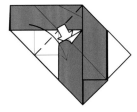

11. Fold the opposite corner over and beneath the folded edge.

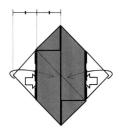

12. Fold the outer corners in and tuck them beneath the upper layer of the middle section.

13. Fold and unfold the upper and lower corners.

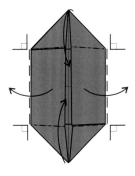

14. Fold the sides out to stand perpendicular to the base.

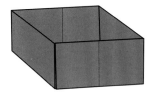

15. Complete.

CLASSIC DESIGNS

Masu Box

*

The Masu box is a traditional design, with its origins thought to be in Japan. The box works by folding the corners of a square to the middle. The folded edges fold in and tuck inside each other to become the walls of the box.

18 X 18CM (7 X 7IN)

x1

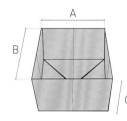

A 6.5cm (2½in)
B 6.5cm (2½in)
C 3cm (1⅛in)

START WITH A SQUARE, COLOURED SIDE UP.

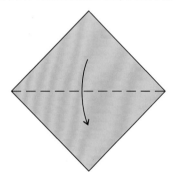

1) Fold the square in half diagonally.

2) Fold the section back up again.

3) Fold and unfold the square along the opposite axis. Then turn the model over, left to right.

4) Fold and unfold the square in half lengthwise.

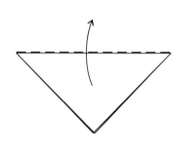

5) Fold all of the corners in to the middle.

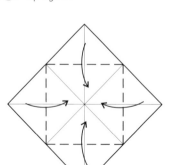

6) Fold the edges in to the middle, then unfold.

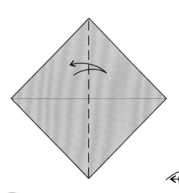

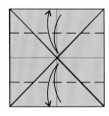

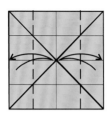
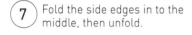

(7) Fold the side edges in to the middle, then unfold.

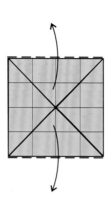

(8) Fold the upper and lower corners out.

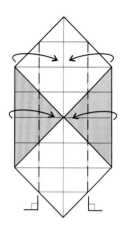

(9) Fold the edges of the model in on both sides to be perpendicular to the base.

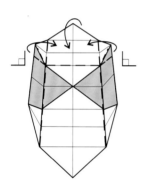

(10) Fold the outer corners in causing the rear section to fold up and lie perpendicular to the base and the edges.

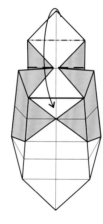

(11) Fold the far point over and into the model.

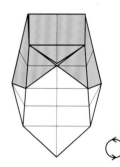

180°

(12) Rotate the model 180°.

(10–11)

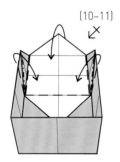

(13) Fold the rear section up and repeat step 10 to 11.

(14) Fold the point into the model.

(15) Complete.

Standing Box One and Two

*

The Standing box is another traditional Japanese design. In this model the box space is supported by the outer edges of the square. There are two versions, one with a supporting edge and the second with legs. The box starts out as a flat model that opens out in the final assembly.

18 X 18CM (7 X 7IN)

x1

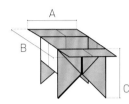

A 4.5cm   (1¾in)
B 9cm   (3½in)
C 4.5cm   (1¾in)

A 4.5cm   (1¾in)
B 9cm   (3½in)
C 4.5cm   (1¾in)

START WITH A SQUARE, COLOURED SIDE UP.

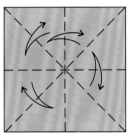

1) Fold and unfold the square in half lengthwise and diagonally along both axes. Then turn the model over, left to right.

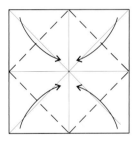

2) Fold the corners in to the middle.

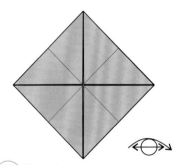

3) Turn the model over, left to right.

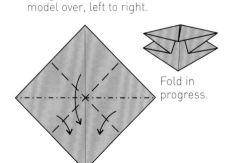

Fold in progress.

4) Fold the upper section down and fold in the outer edges to form a preliminary base.

180°

5) Rotate the model by 180°.

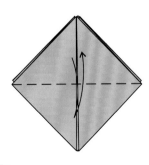

6) Fold and unfold the upper layer in half.

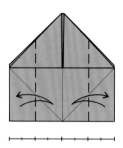

Fold in progress.

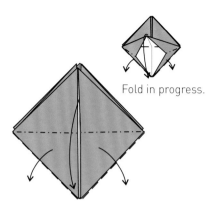

(7) Fold the upper layer down and fold out and open up the lower section.

(8) Fold and unfold the upper layer of the outer edges in to the middle.

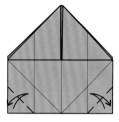

(9) Fold and unfold the outer lower corners in to the creases on both sides.

(10) Fold the lower edge up to the folded edge above, causing the lower corners to fold in.

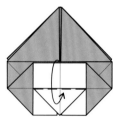

(11) Fold the upper edge down and behind the lower layer.

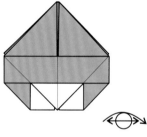

(12) Turn the model over, left to right.

[6–11]

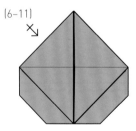

(13) Repeat steps 6 to 11.

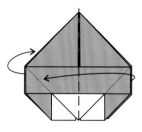

(14) Fold one side over, on both the front and back.

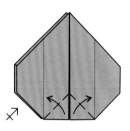

(15) Fold the inner corners up to the adjacent creases. Repeat behind.

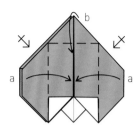
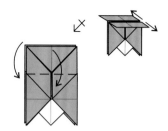

16 Fold the sides in at (a) then fold the upper corners over at (b). Repeat behind.

17 Fold the upper edge over. Repeat behind. Hold the two upper tabs and pull apart to open the model

18 Complete.

STANDING BOX TWO

START WITH A SQUARE, COLOURED SIDE UP, START WITH STEP 8 OF STANDING BOX ONE AND REPEAT STEP 7 BEHIND.

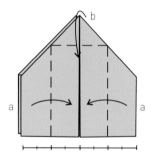
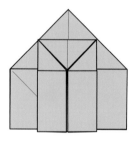
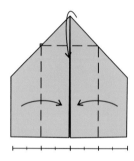

1 Fold the sides in at (a) then fold the upper corner over at (b).

2 Turn the model over, left to right.

3 Repeat step 1 and fold in the sides and the upper corner.

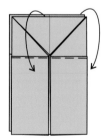
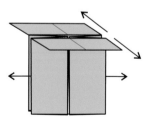
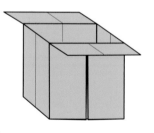

4 Fold the upper edge over to lie perpendicular to the base front and behind.

5 Hold the two upper tabs and pull apart to open the model.

6 Complete.

Ginger Jar

**

The Ginger jar is thought to be a traditional Chinese model.
It works by building a flat model that can be opened out in the final assembly.

18 X 18CM (7 X 7IN)

x1

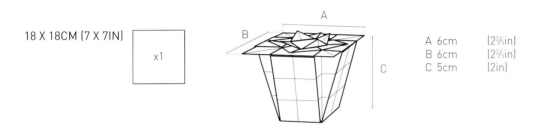

A 6cm (2⅖in)
B 6cm (2⅖in)
C 5cm (2in)

START WITH A SQUARE, COLOURED SIDE UP.

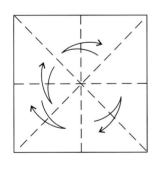

1 Fold and unfold the square in half diagonally and lengthwise. Then turn the model over, left to right.

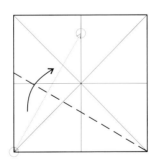

2 Fold the lower corner up to touch the middle crease.

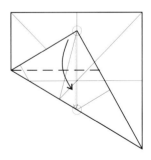

3 Fold the edge of the folded section down to touch the folded edge.

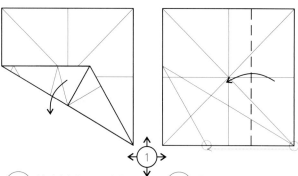

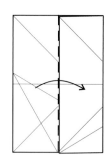

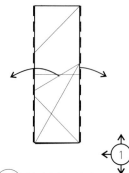

(4) Unfold the model back to a square.

(5) Fold one side in to enable the opposite lower corner to touch the crease made previously.

(6) Fold the other side over.

(7) Unfold back to a square.

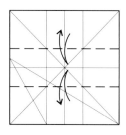

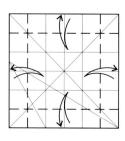

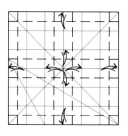

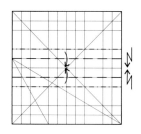

(8) Fold and unfold the upper and lower edges at the point where the creases intersect.

(9) Fold and unfold between the outer edges and the creases made previously.

(10) Fold and unfold between the outer edges and the creases made previously.

(11) Fold the upper and lower sections in and out again, making two zigzag folds.

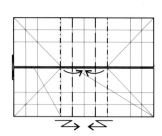

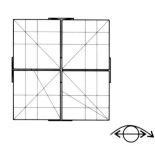

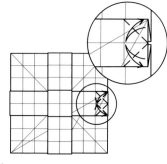

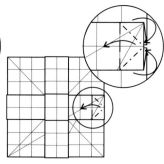

(12) Fold the outer side sections in and out again, making two zigzag folds.

(13) Turn the model over, left to right.

(14) Fold and unfold the corners of the inner section.

(15) Fold the edge of the section over and fold and squash the outer corners.

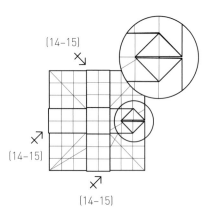

(14–15)

(14–15)

(14–15)

16 Repeat steps 14 to 15 on the other three sections.

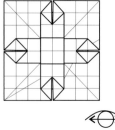

17 Turn the model over, left to right.

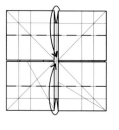

18 Fold the upper and lower edges in to the middle.

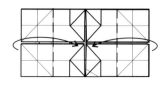

19 Fold the two sides to the middle and slide them underneath the middle section.

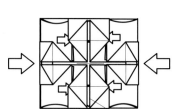

20 Continue folding the edges in and tuck them into the middle section.

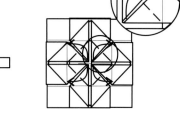

21 Fold the inner corners out.

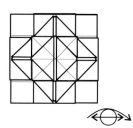

22 Turn the model over, left to right.

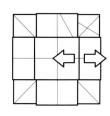

23 Open out the paper trapped inside the middle section by sliding the edges apart.

24 Continue sliding the layers apart.

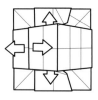

25 Repeat this process on the other three sides.

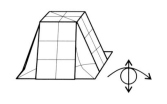

26 Shape the sides of the jar. Then turn the model over, top to bottom.

27 Complete.

Lazy Susan

*

A lazy Susan is a serving dish with multiple compartments. The model forms box sections by inverting the inner edge of four folded pockets. This process creates a rounded edge.

18 X 18CM (7 X 7IN)   x1

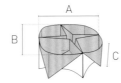

A 7.5cm   (3in)
B 7.5cm   (3in)
C 3.25cm   (1⅓in)

START WITH A SQUARE, COLOURED SIDE UP.

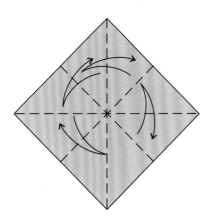

(1) Fold and unfold the square in half diagonally along both axes.

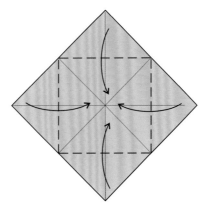

(2) Fold the corners in to the middle.

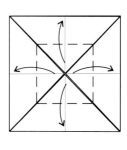

(3) Fold the corners out to touch the middle of the outer edges.

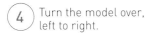

(4) Turn the model over, left to right.

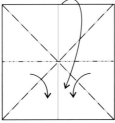

Fold in progress.

(5) Fold the upper section down; at the same time fold in the edges to make a waterbomb base.

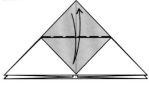

(6) Fold and unfold the upper corner along the adjacent folded edge.

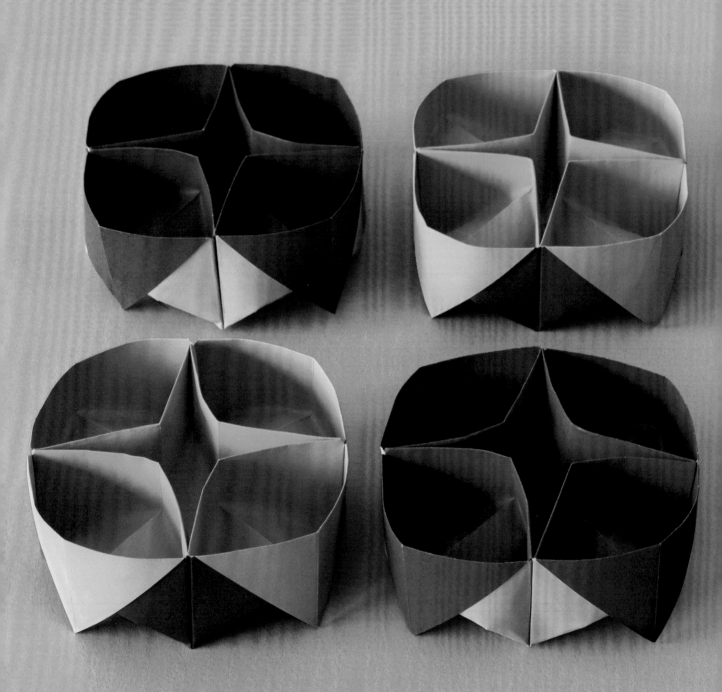

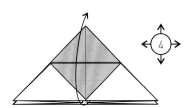

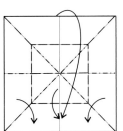

⑦ Fold the lower edge up and open the model.

⑧ Fold the upper section down and the sides in. At the same time, reverse fold the inner square into the model.

⑨ Fold and unfold the outer corners. Repeat behind.

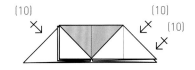

⑩ Reverse fold the corner inside the model.

⑪ Repeat the process (step 10) and reverse fold all of the corners inside.

⑫ Fold the front and reverse sections to be perpendicular to the middle section.

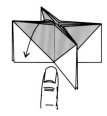
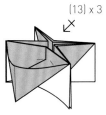

⑬ Pull the front layer of the section forward and open it out.

⑭ Repeat this opening process on the other three sides. Then round and shape the box.

⑮ Complete.

Star Box

*

The Star box is a contemporary design, a standing box formed by folding in the corners of a waterbomb base. Again the folding process makes a flat model that opens out to become three-dimensional; the corners of the square become legs that support the box.

18 X 18CM (7 X 7IN)

x1

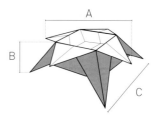

A	9.5cm	(3¾in)
B	4cm	(1⅔in)
C	9.5cm	(3¾in)

START WITH A SQUARE, COLOURED SIDE UP.

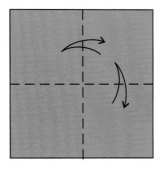

1. Fold and unfold the square in half lengthwise along both axes.

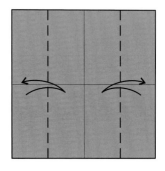

2. Fold and unfold the side edges in to the middle crease.

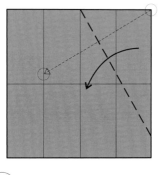

3. Fold the upper corner in to touch the adjacent vertical crease. The fold should start from the middle crease.

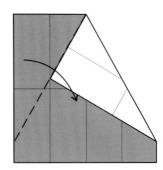

4. Fold the other upper corner over the folded section.

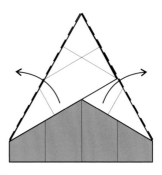

5. Fold the corners back out.

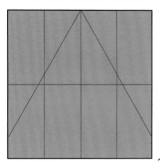

6. Turn the model over, left to right.

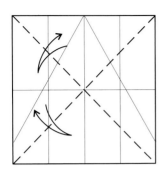

(7) Fold and unfold the square diagonally along both axes.

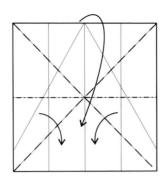

(8) Fold the upper section down and fold the sides in, forming a waterbomb base.

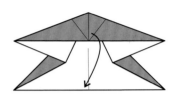

(9) Fold in progress.

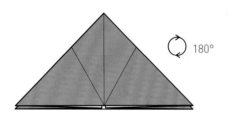

180°

(10) Rotate the model by 180°.

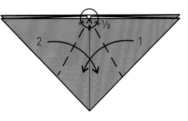

(11) Fold the two outer corners in along the creases made previously.

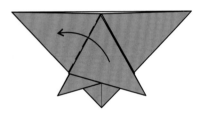

(12) Fold one corner back out.

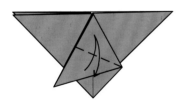

(13) Fold and unfold the section in half.

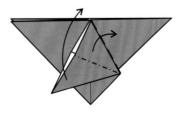

(14) Fold the section up, separate the layers and squash the point flat.

(15) Fold and unfold the outer edges to the crease.

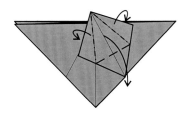

16. Fold the corner back between the creases. This will cause the upper edges to fold in.

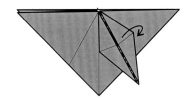

17. Fold the edge of the section behind.

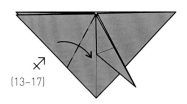

(13–17)

18. Fold the opposite corner over and repeat steps 13 to 17.

19. Turn the model over, left to right.

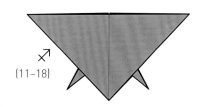

(11–18)

20. Repeat steps 11 to 18. The folds in step 11 should be aligned with the folded edge behind.

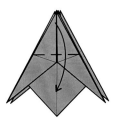

21. Fold the front upper corner down.

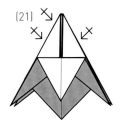

(21)

22. Repeat step 21 on the other three upper corners.

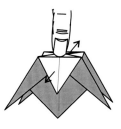

23. Open out the model and shape the base.

24. Complete.

MODERN BOXES

Juno
**

Juno has a similar structure to the traditional Masu box (see page 14). Both boxes have a similar central section. However, the corners that fold in on the Masu box are here woven together to close the box.

18 X 18CM (7 X 7IN) x1

A 6.5cm (2½in)
B 6.5cm (2½in)
C 3.1cm (1⅛in)

START WITH A SQUARE, COLOURED SIDE UP.

1) Fold and unfold the square in half diagonally along both axes. Then turn the model over, left to right.

2) Fold and unfold the square lengthwise along both axes.

3) Fold and unfold the corners in to the middle.

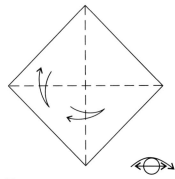

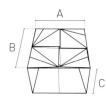

Fold in progress.

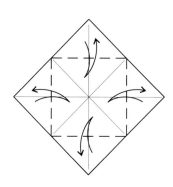

4) Fold the upper section down and fold the sides in to make a preliminary base.

5) Fold the corners in to the middle on all sides and unfold.

6) Fold the outer edges in diagonally to touch the adjacent crease. Crease, then unfold.

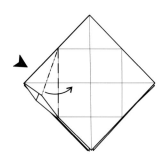

7 Fold the corner up, separate the layers and squash the point flat.

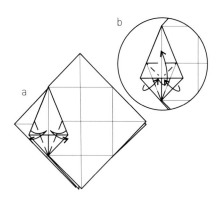

8 (a) Fold the outer edges in to the middle, crease then unfold. (b) Then fold up the edge of the squashed section refolding (a).

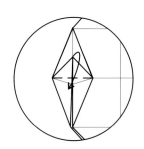

9 Fold the point down.

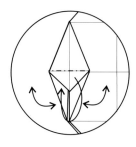

10 Pull the lower points apart and fold the inner corner behind and into the model.

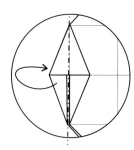

11 Fold the outer side behind.

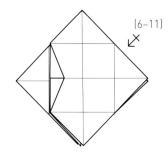

12 Repeat steps 6 to 11 on the other side.

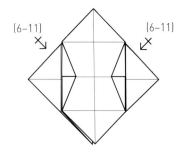

13 Repeat steps 6 to 11 on the two corners of the rear section.

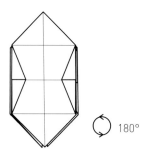

14 Rotate the model by 180°.

15 Fold the upper corner down.

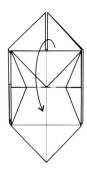

16 Fold the upper section down again.

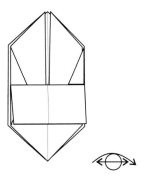

17 Turn the model over, left to right.

18 Fold the upper point over, then over again.

19 Fold the upper face to the right and the reverse face to the left to expose the hidden faces.

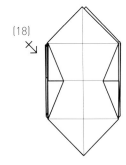

20 Repeat the folds in step 18 on the front and behind to fold the upper sections down and over again.

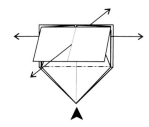

21 Pull the tabs out to open the model and flatten the base.

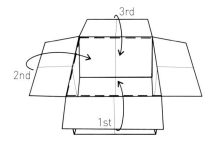

22 Fold the upper tabs in, one after the other, in number order, to lie flat on top of the model.

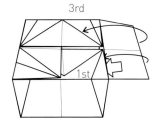

23 Fold the final tab it. It should tuck underneath the first tab and sit on top of the third.

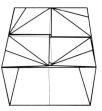

24 The lid should fit together and close to complete the model.

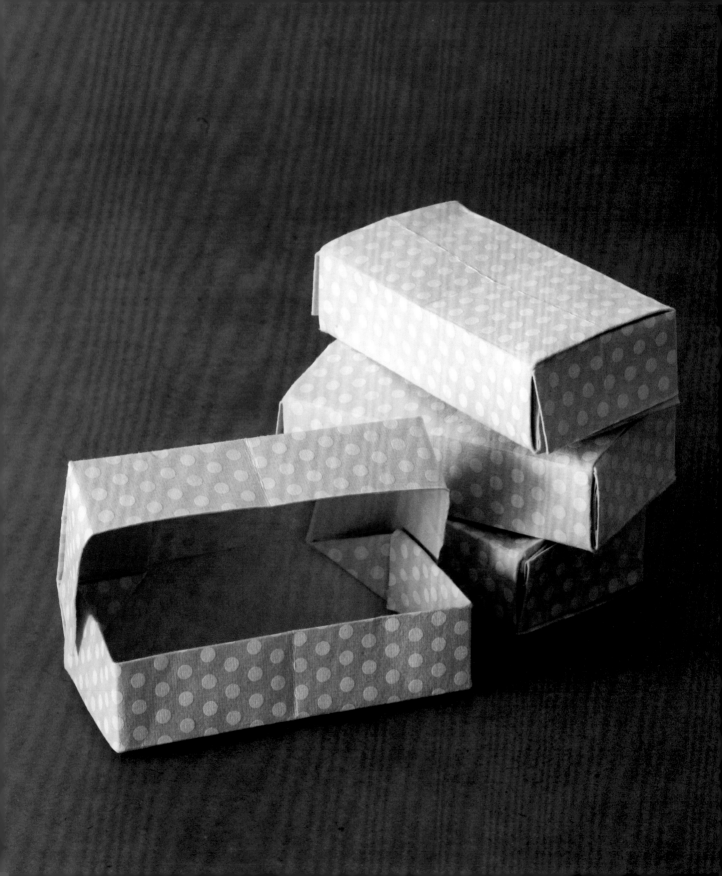

Launce

*

The Launce is made by transforming a square into two similar shaped sides that fold into each other. The two sections fit neatly in to each other to close the box.

18 X 18CM (7 X 7IN)

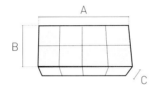

A 9cm   (3½in)
B 4.5cm   (1¾in)
C 2.25cm (9/10in)

START WITH A SQUARE, COLOURED SIDE UP.

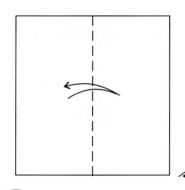

1 Fold and unfold the square in half lengthwise. Then turn the model over, left to right.

2 Fold the edges in to the middle crease and unfold.

3 Repeat steps 1–2 on the opposite axis to fold the square into four sections lengthwise.

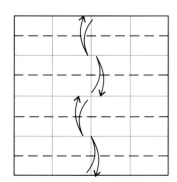

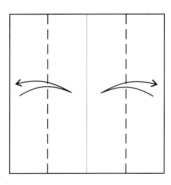

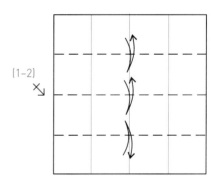

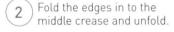

4 Fold and unfold between the creases on one axis.

5 Fold and unfold the outer edges in to the adjacent creases.

6 Fold the lower section up along the first horizontal crease.

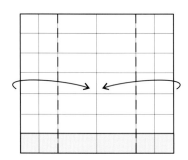

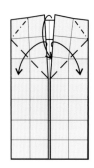

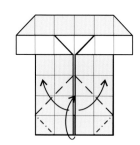

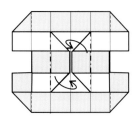

(7) Fold the outer edges in to the middle crease.

(8) Fold the upper section down and fold out the front layers on both sides to open out the upper section.

(9) Fold the lower section up and open it out by folding the inner edges up to the horizontal crease.

(10) Fold the inner edges behind and into the model.

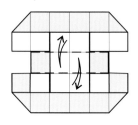

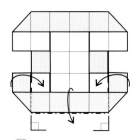

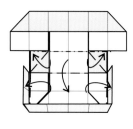

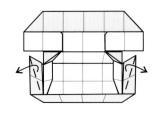

(11) Fold and unfold along the horizontal creases as shown.

(12) Fold the lower edge out to stand perpendicular to the base. The outer edges will fold in too.

(13) Fold the inner sections up to lie next to the perpendicular edges.

(14) Fold the upper layer of the inner folded edges up slightly.

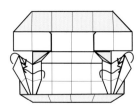

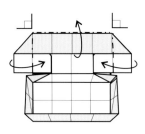

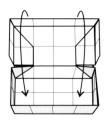

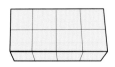

(15) Fold the edges in and tuck them into the outer edges. Then fold the layers back down again.

(16) Fold the edge up to open the lid and make the edges stand perpendicular to the base.

(17) Fold the lid over to close the box.

(18) Complete.

Oberon

✳ ✳ ✳

Oberon is an eight-sided box. The edges and corners of the square fold in and lock together to close the box.

18 X 18CM (7 X 7IN)

A 7.2cm   (2⅘in)
B 7.2cm   (2⅘in)
C 3cm   (1⅕in)

START WITH A SQUARE, COLOURED SIDE UP.

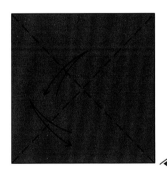

1. Fold and unfold the square in half diagonally. Then turn the paper over, left to right.

2. Fold and unfold the square in half lengthwise.

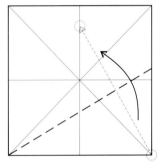

3. Fold the lower right corner up to touch the vertical middle crease, folding from the lower left corner.

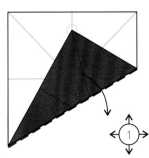

4. Unfold the previous step.

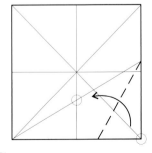

5. Fold lower corner in to touch the crease made previously.

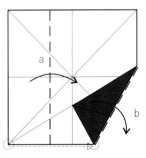

6. Fold the left side in (a), then unfold the corner folded over in the previous step (b).

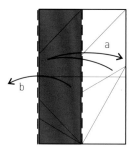

7 (a) Fold the outer side in and out again. Then (b) Unfold back to a square.

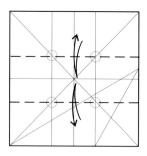

8 Fold the upper and lower edges in where the vertical creases touch the diagonal folds, to divide it into thirds.

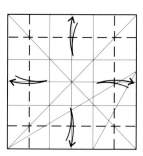

9 Fold and unfold the outer edges in to touch the adjacent creases. Rotate the paper by 45°.

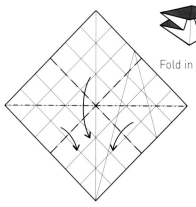

Fold in progress.

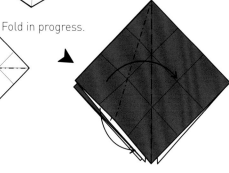

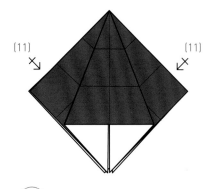

10 Fold the upper section down; at the same time fold in the outer corners to make a preliminary base.

11 Fold the left corner up, separate the layers and squash flat.

12 Repeat step 11 on all faces to squash the other three corners.

13 Fold and unfold the upper point along the creases made previously.

14 Fold the upper layer over on one side. The fold should start where the upper crease touches the edge.

15 Fold the section back again.

(16) Fold the upper face to the right, and the rear face to the left, to expose the adjacent faces.

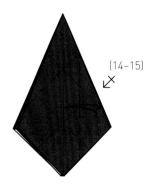

(14–15)

(17) Fold the edge over and unfold, repeating steps 14 to 15.

(16–17) x 6

(18) Repeat steps 16 to 17 on the other six faces. All of the corners should fold in the same direction.

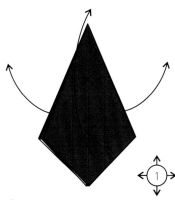

(19) Open the model up to form a square.

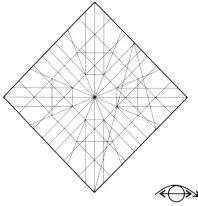

(20) Turn the model over, left to right.

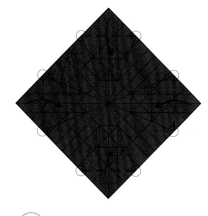

(21) Fold the corners in where the creases touch the edge of the square.

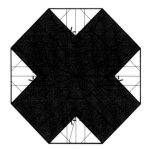

(22) Fold the tips of the folded corners behind, aligned with the crease beneath.

(23) Make a series of diagonal creases around the edge of the model.

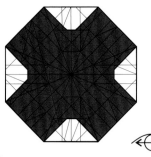

(24) Turn the paper over, left to right.

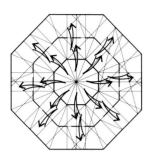

(25) Fold and unfold along the creases made previously to reinforce the folds in the base and upper edge.

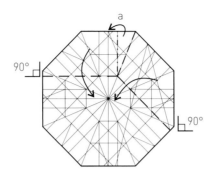

(26) Fold two edges up to be perpendicular to the base. The triangle (a) will fold behind.

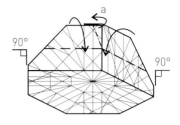

(27) Fold the two upper edges down to lie parallel to the base. At the same time, make the diagonal fold at (a).

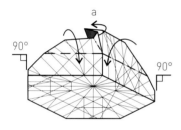

(28) This shows the fold (step 27) in progress.

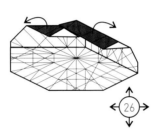

(29) Unfold the previous folds to step 26. The next steps will repeat this process simultaneously on all sides.

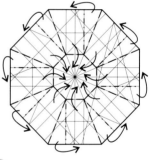

(30) Fold all sides in so they are perpendicular to the base. At the same time, fold the adjacent triangles behind.

(31) Fold the upper edges in to the middle, repeating step 27 to 28 on all sides.

(32) The upper section should all fold together. Fold the edges behind to lock these in place.

(33) Complete.

Feste

**

The base of the Feste box is formed by a series of parallel diagonal folds that fold in to one other. The upper edges of the model weave together to close the top.

18 X 18CM (7 X 7IN)

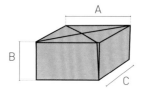

A 6.5cm (2½in)
B 3.5cm (1⅖in)
C 6.5cm (2½in)

START WITH A SQUARE, COLOURED SIDE UP.

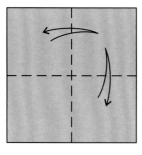

(1) Fold and unfold the square in half lengthwise. Then turn the paper over, left to right.

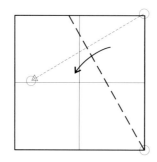

(2) Fold a corner in to touch the horizontal crease. The fold should start from the lower right corner.

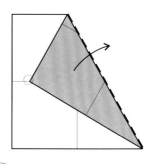

(3) Unfold the previous step.

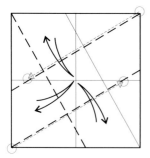

(4) Fold and unfold the other three corners in, repeating step 3. Then turn the model over, left to right.

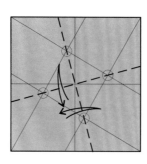

(5) Fold and unfold two diagonal folds through the intersections of the creases. Then turn the model over, left to right.

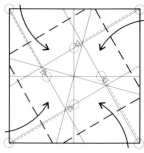

(6) Fold the corners in to make them touch the intersections of the vertical and horizontal creases.

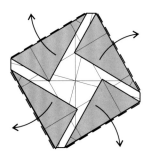

(7) Unfold the previous step.

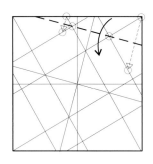

(8) Fold the upper edge over to make the upper right corner touch the crease. The fold should go through the intersection of the creases as shown.

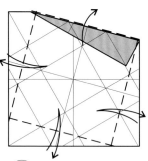

(9) Unfold the corner. Then repeat the process (step 8) on the other three corners.

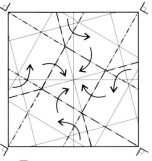

(10) Fold the four sides in to stand perpendicular to the base by refolding the creases made previously.

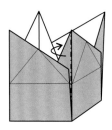

(11) Fold the edge behind and flatten it against the adjacent section.

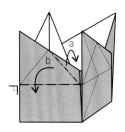

(12) Fold the edge (a) behind. Then fold the corner (b) down to lie perpendicular to the lower section.

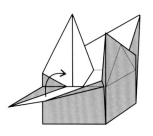

(13) Fold the corner back up again, maintaining the creased edge.

(11–13) x 3

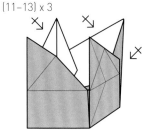

(14) Repeat steps 11 to 13 on the other three corners.

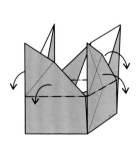

(15) Fold all of the corners out to lie perpendicular to the sides.

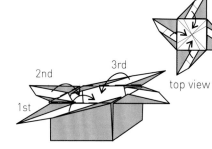

(16) Fold the corners in, in the sequence shown, so that each corner covers the one folded previously.

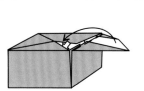

(17) Fold the final corner over and tuck the point beneath the first folded corner. This locks the upper section together.

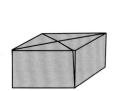

(18) Complete.

Cobweb
✳✳

The Cobweb box is made using a similar geometry to the Feste box (see page 46). However, the sides are shallower, with the excess paper being used to make a decorative lid. The four upper corners fold in together to make a star-shaped pattern.

18 X 18CM (7 X 7IN)

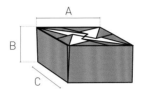

A 6.75cm   (2²⁄₃in)
B 2.63cm   (1in)
C 6.75cm   (2²⁄₃in)

START WITH A SQUARE, COLOURED SIDE UP.

1 Fold and unfold the square in half lengthwise. Then turn the paper over, left to right.

2 Fold and unfold each of the corners in to touch the vertical and horizontal creases. Then turn the model over, left to right.

3 Fold and unfold the square diagonally through the intersection of the creases.

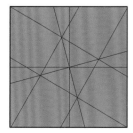

4 Turn the model over, left to right.

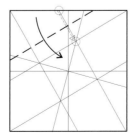

5 Fold the corner in parallel to the crease. The outer upper edge should touch the intersection of the creases.

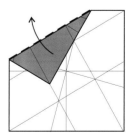

6 Unfold the previous step.

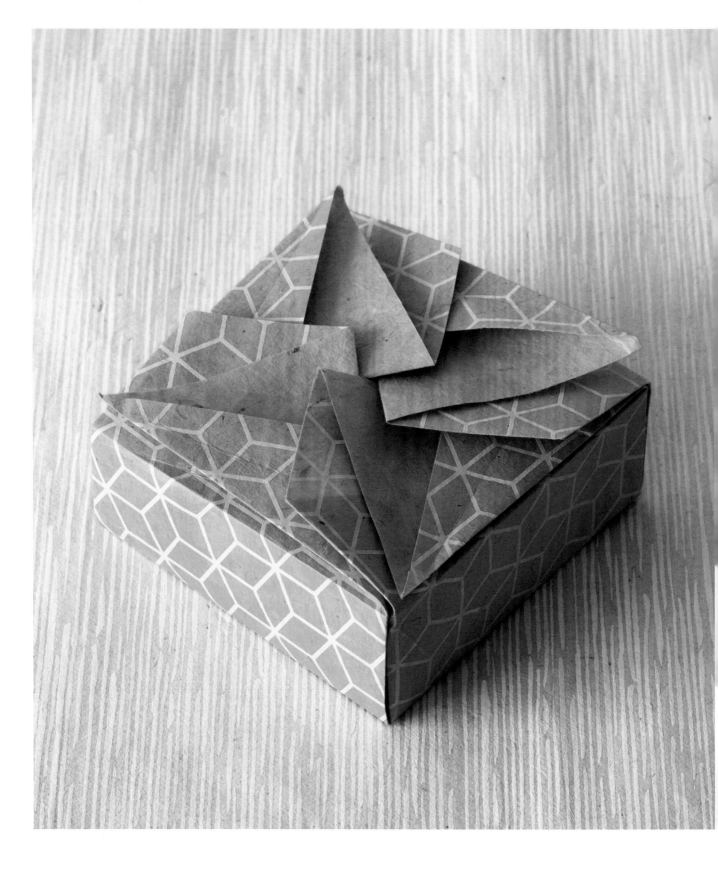

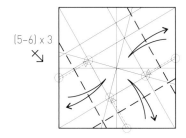

(5–6) x 3

(7) Repeat step 5 to 6 on the other three corners.

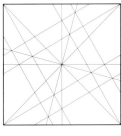

(8) Turn the model over, left to right.

(9) Fold and unfold the corners to touch the vertical and horizontal creases. The folds should start from the opposite corners. Then turn the model over, left to right.

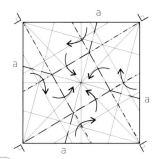

a

a

a

a

(10) Fold the corners up to stand perpendicular to the base and, at the same time, fold in the paper (a) inside

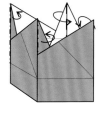

(11) Fold the edges behind so that they lie next to the outer edges.

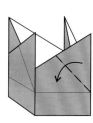

(12) Fold the corner over along the crease made previously.

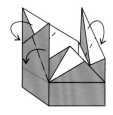

(13) Fold the other three corners over.

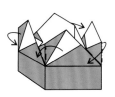

(14) Fold the four corners in simultaneously so they all fit together.

top view.

(15) Complete.

Pinch

*

The Pinch is based on the shape of a square-bottomed bag. The sides of the model fold in and concertina together, then the final closure is achieved by folding a flap over and into the model. This holds the inner layers together and closes the box.

18 X 18CM (7 X 7IN)   x1

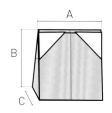

A 6cm   (2⅓in)
B 6cm   (2⅓in)
C 3cm   (1⅕in)

START WITH A SQUARE, COLOURED SIDE UP.

(1) Fold and unfold the square in half lengthwise and diagonally along both axes. Then turn the paper over, left to right.

(2) Fold and unfold the upper right corner between the upper left corner and the middle crease.

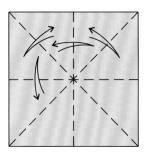

(3) Fold and unfold the lower edge to the intersection of the creases above.

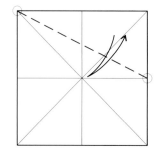

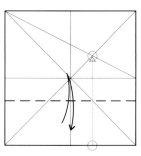

(4) Fold the right edge in along a vertical line that goes though the intersection of the creases.

(5) Fold the lower right corner to the right by making a diagonal fold above that causes the lower edge to fold up.

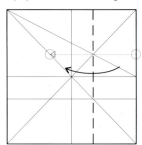

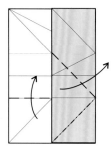

(6) Fold the corner up, separate the layers and squash the point flat.

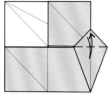

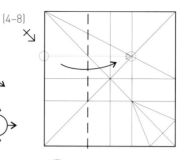

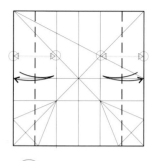

(7) Fold the tip of the squashed section down and unfold.

(8) Unfold the model back to a square.

(9) Repeat steps 4 to 8 on the other side, starting by folding the opposite side in.

(10) Fold and unfold the outer edges in to the adjacent creases.

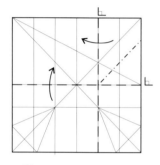

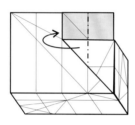

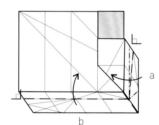

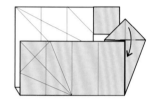

(11) Fold the front section up and the side in. The sides should lie perpendicular to one another.

(12) Fold the edge behind.

(13) Fold the edge in at (a), then fold the front section (b) up and on top of it.

(14) Fold the triangular point down over the folded edge.

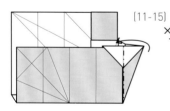

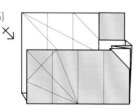

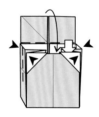

(15) Reverse fold the corner inside the model.

(16) Repeat steps 11 to 15 on the other side.

(17) Squeeze the upper section together and fold the upper edge over and tuck it behind the front face, into the model.

(18) Complete.

Nym

The Nym box folds the paper around a box shape. Following the diagonal axis of the paper, the model is closed by folding a corner of the square into a pocket. This locks the box together to make a satisfying block shape.

18 X 18CM (7 X 7IN)   x1

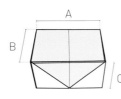

A 6.3cm   (2½in)
B 3.15cm   (1¼in)
C 3.15cm   (1¼in)

START WITH A SQUARE, COLOURED SIDE UP.

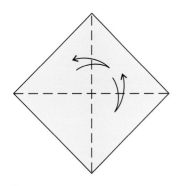

(1) Fold and unfold the square in half diagonally.

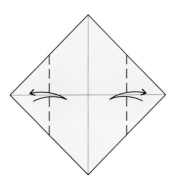

(2) Fold the outer corners in to touch the centre. Unfold.

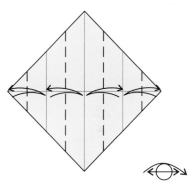

(3) Fold between the creases made previously and unfold. Turn the model over, left to right.

(2-3)

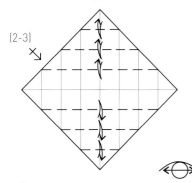

(4) Repeat steps 2 to 3 along the other axis. Then turn the model over, left to right.

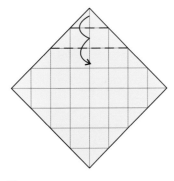

(5) Fold the upper corner over, then over again.

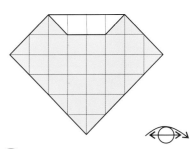

(6) Turn the model over, left to right.

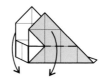

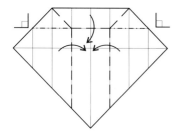

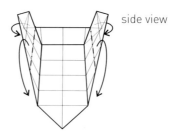

side view

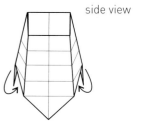

side view

7) Fold the rear section and sides up to stand perpendicular to the base of the model and pinch together the outer corners.

8) Fold the rear corners in to be flush with the sides. Then fold the sides down.

9) Fold the lower corners to be flattened to the base.

side view.

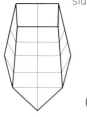

180°

side view.

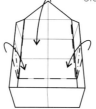

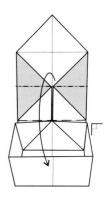

10) Rotate the model by 180° to look at the back of the model.

11) Fold the sides of the rear section in, causing the whole rear section to fold up perpendicular to the base.

12) Fold the lid over the rear edge.

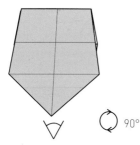

90°

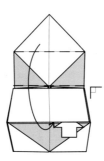

13) Rotate the model vertically by 90°. The next step will show the front side of the model.

14) Fold the upper section over against the upper face of the model and tuck the corner into the pocket.

15) Complete.

TWO-PIECE BOXES

Saru

*

Based on the same principles as the Feste and Coweb boxes (see pages 46 and 49). The lid and the base are made in a similar way. The lid should be made from a square that is slightly larger than the square used for the base.

18 X 18CM (7 X 7IN)

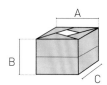

A 6.75cm (2⅔in)
B 5.20cm (2in)
C 6.75cm (2⅔in)

START WITH A SQUARE, COLOURED SIDE UP.

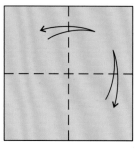

(1) Fold and unfold the square in half lengthwise. Then turn the paper over, left to right.

(2) Fold the lower corner up to touch the vertical crease. The fold should start from the opposite corner.

(3) Unfold the previous step.

[2–3]

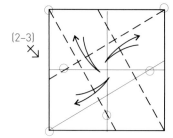

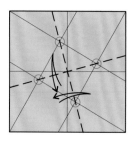

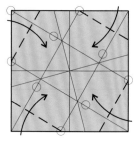

(4) Repeat steps 2 to 3 on the other axes. Then turn the model over, left to right.

(5) Fold and unfold between the creases. Note the reference points are the intersection of the creases.

(6) Fold the corners in parallel to the creases made previously, starting where the creases touch the edges.

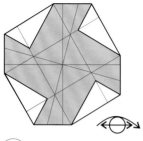

7 Turn the model over, left to right.

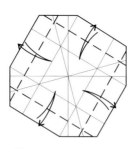

8 Fold and unfold the outer edges to the adjacent creases.

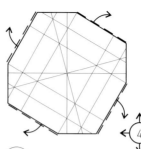

9 Unfold back to a square, (step 4), by folding the corners out from behind.

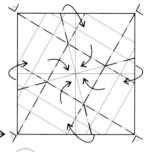

10 Fold the sides up and the edges in, along the creases made previously.

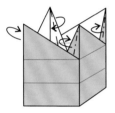

11 Fold the edges of the triangles behind.

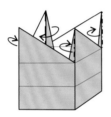

12 Fold the edges over again to lie flat against the adjacent corners.

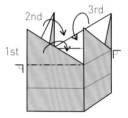

13 Fold the corners in on top of each other following the order as shown.

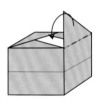

14 Fold the final corner in and tuck it beneath the first folded corner.

LID

15 Complete.

1 Lid: with a slightly larger square fold to step 11 and fold the corners down.

2 Fold the upper section down and into the model.

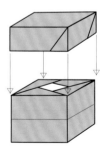

3 Place the lid on the base to complete the model.

Orinoco
✳✳

The Orinoco is an octagonal box, with the base and lid being made from similar-sized squares. The model shown is made from a map of the world and shows how different patterns and designs can be used to good effect.

18 X 18CM (7 X 7IN)

x1

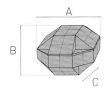

A 10.8cm (4¼in)
B 10.8cm (4¼in)
C 9cm (3½in)

START WITH A SQUARE, COLOURED SIDE UP.

(1) Fold and unfold the square in half lengthwise along both axes. Turn paper over, left to right.

(2) Fold and unfold the edges to the middle crease.

(3) Fold and unfold between the creases made previously.

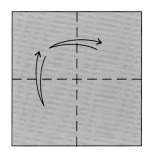

[2-3]

(4) Repeat steps 2 to 3 on the other axis. Then turn the model over, left to right.

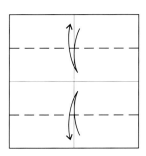
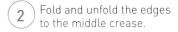
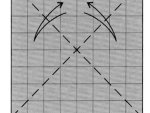

(5) Fold and unfold diagonally along the middle. Then turn the model over, left to right.

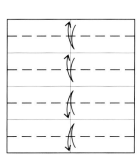

(6) Fold the sides (a) up to be perpendicular to the base and fold in the corner (b).

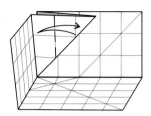

7 Fold and unfold the folded corner along the second crease.

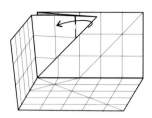

8 Fold the corner over along the first crease.

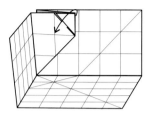

9 Fold the corner over again.

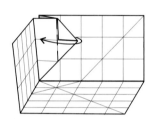

10 Fold the section over.

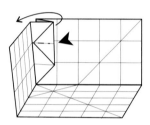

11 Push the section out, leaving an inverted pyramid on the lower layer.

(6–11) x 3

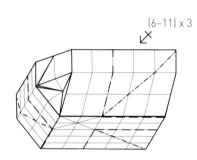

12 Repeat steps 6 to 11 on the other three sides.

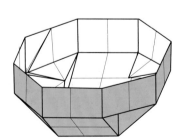

13 Base section complete.

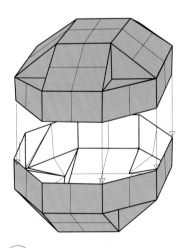

14 Make a second 'bowl' and insert into the first.

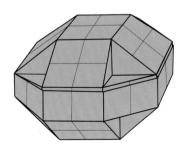

15 Complete.

Doki

**

Doki emerges from a hexagon folded in the middle of the square. The double-layered sides are made by folding the edges of the square around the central shape. The square used for the lid should be slightly smaller than the one used for the base.

LID   18 X 18CM (7 X 7IN)

x1

BASE   17 X 17CM (6²/₃ X 6²/₃IN)

x1

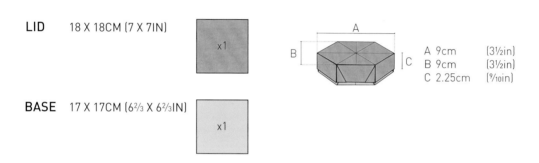

A 9cm	(3½in)
B 9cm	(3½in)
C 2.25cm	(⁹/₁₀in)

LID: START WITH A SQUARE, COLOURED SIDE UP.

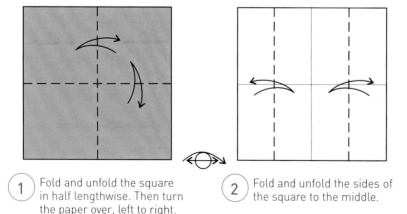

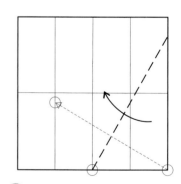

1 Fold and unfold the square in half lengthwise. Then turn the paper over, left to right.

2 Fold and unfold the sides of the square to the middle.

3 Fold the corner of the square in to touch the crease. The fold will start from the middle crease.

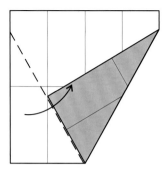

(4) Fold the opposite side over the folded edge.

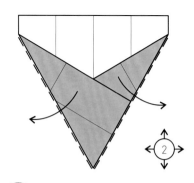

(5) Unfold back to a square.

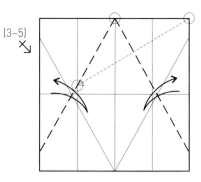

(6) Repeat steps 3 to 5 on the upper section.

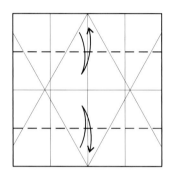

(7) Fold and unfold the upper and lower edges to the middle.

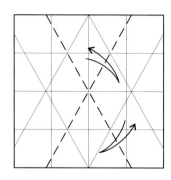

(8) Fold and unfold between the diagonal creases made previously.

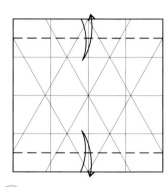

(9) Fold and unfold the upper and lower edges to the adjacent creases.

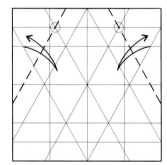

(10) Fold and unfold the corners along a line parallel to the inner diagonal crease. Note the reference points at 'O'.

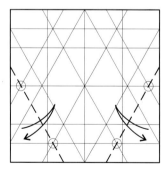

(11) Fold and unfold the corners in. The folds should cut through the two crease intersections (the two 'O's).

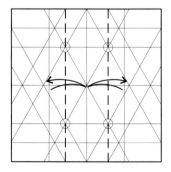

(12) Fold and unfold vertically where indicated. Note the reference points at 'O'.

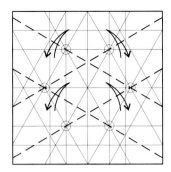

13 Fold and unfold where shown. Each crease is folded where the creases intersect.

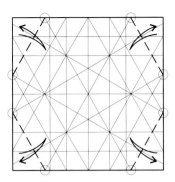

14 Fold and unfold the corners between the points where the creases touch the edge of the square. (The two 'O's).

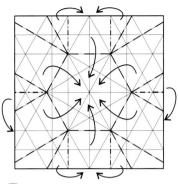

15 Fold the sides up around the hexagon shape in the middle.

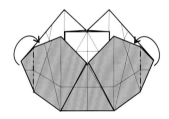

16 Reverse fold the corners inside the model and flatten them to the edge inside.

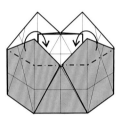

17 Fold the upper edge behind and into the model.

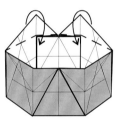

18 Fold the rear edges over and into the model.

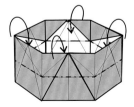

19 Fold the whole edge over and into the model. This should lock the lid together.

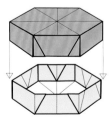

20 The lid and the base are made in the same way. For a good fit, make the base from a slightly smaller square. Place the lid on the base.

21 Complete.

Indus

**

The Indus box starts by dividing the paper into five equal sections. The first and the fifth sections tuck into one another to form a four-sided tube shape. The corners of the square fold in and seal the base. The lid is made in a similar way.

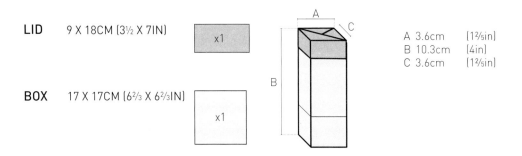

LID   9 X 18CM (3½ X 7IN)   x1

BOX   17 X 17CM (6⅔ X 6⅔IN)   x1

A 3.6cm   (1⅖in)
B 10.3cm   (4in)
C 3.6cm   (1⅖in)

The height of the box can be varied by changing the dimensions of the starting rectangle. The lid for the Indus is made in a similar way to the box, with a rectangle made from half a square. The starting square should be slightly wider (about 1 cm/½in) than the square used for the base.

BASE

START WITH A SQUARE, COLOURED SIDE UP.

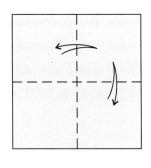

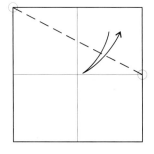

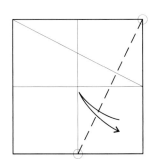

1. Fold and unfold the square in half lengthwise along both axes. Turn the paper over, left to right.

2. Fold and unfold diagonally between the upper corner and the middle crease.

3. Fold and unfold between the upper right corner and the lower middle crease.

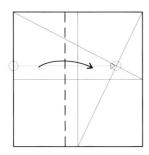

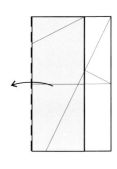

(4) Fold the left side in to touch the point where the two creases touch.

(5) Fold and unfold the right edge over the folded edge.

(6) Unfold back to a square.

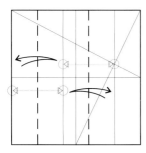

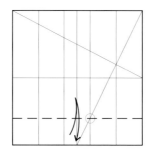

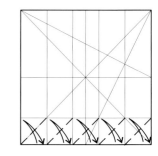

(7) Fold and unfold between the creases to divide the paper into five equal sections.

(8) Fold and unfold horizontally at the point where the vertical crease touches the diagonal crease.

(9) Fold and unfold a series of diagonal valley folds between the corners of the lower squares.

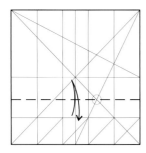

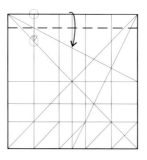

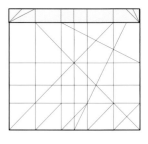

(10) Fold and unfold horizontally. The crease should go through the point where the two creases intersect.

(11) Fold the upper section down to the point where the creases intersect. Adjusting this crease will enable the box to be longer or shorter.

(12) Turn the paper over, left to right.

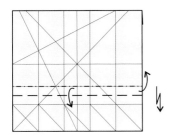

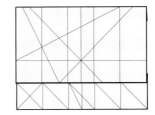

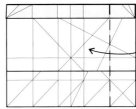

(13) Fold the upper section down and up again, making a zigzag fold.

(14) Turn the paper over, left to right.

(15) Fold the right side in.

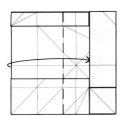

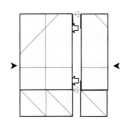

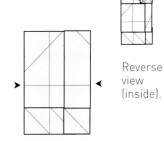

Reverse view (inside).

(16) Fold the left side in along the second crease and tuck one side into the other.

(17) When sliding the two sides into each other, the left section should fold inside the right section.

(18) Slide in progress. Ensure the zigzag fold and the folded upper edge are aligned.

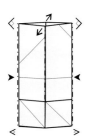

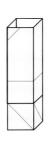

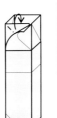

Top view.

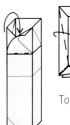

Top view.

(19) Push the sides together to make the four sides perpendicular to each other.

(20) Turn the model over, top to bottom

(21) Fold the inner corner behind, along the crease made previously.

(22) Fold the next edge in, along the diagonal, so the previous edge folds in too.

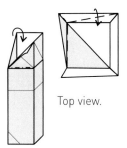

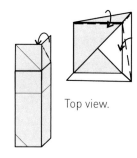

(23) Fold the next corner in, along with the edge folded previously.

(24) Fold the next corner in, along with the edge folded previously.

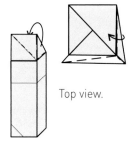

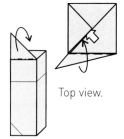

(25) Fold the next corner in, along with the edge folded previously.

(26) Fold the final corner in and tuck the point beneath the edge of the adjacent triangle.

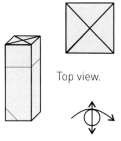

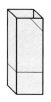

(27) Turn the model over, top to bottom.

(28) Complete.

LID

THE LID IS MADE FROM A 2 X 1 RECTANGLE. THE ORIGINAL MODEL MADE THIS RECTANGLE FROM HALF A SQUARE OF A SIMILAR SIZE TO THE BASE. HOWEVER, WHEN USING THICKER PAPER, THE STARTING SQUARE SHOULD BE SLIGHTLY LARGER.

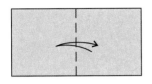

1 Fold and unfold in half lengthwise.

2 Fold and unfold between the right edge and the crease made previously.

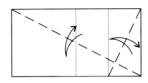

3 Make two diagonal folds between the corners and the creases.

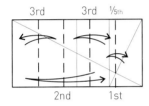

4 Fold horizontally where the creases intersect. Then divide the remaining section into four by folding the outer edge to the crease.

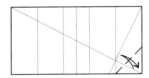

5 Fold and unfold the lower right corner to the adjacent crease.

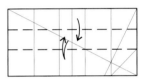

6 Fold the upper edge down to touch the end of the previous diagonal crease. Then fold and unfold the lower section.

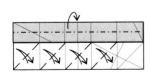

7 Fold the upper edge behind. Then make a series of diagonal folds along the lower section.

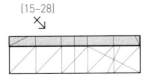

8 Join the two ends together and repeat steps 15 to 28 to complete the smaller lid.

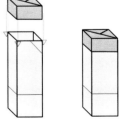

9 The lid should fit on to the box to complete the project.

Lena

**

Lena is a two-piece box with a decorative lid that fits neatly on to a traditional Masu box (see page 14). The lid is folded in a similar way to the Masu box. However, excess paper is used to add decoration. The project shown flattens the top, but it could be left standing as a triangular point.

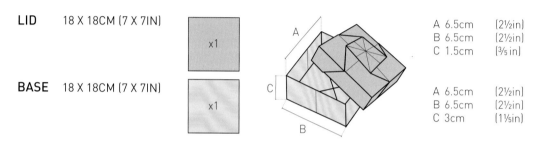

LID	18 X 18CM (7 X 7IN)		A 6.5cm	(2½in)
		x1	B 6.5cm	(2½in)
			C 1.5cm	(⅗in)
BASE	18 X 18CM (7 X 7IN)		A 6.5cm	(2½in)
		x1	B 6.5cm	(2½in)
			C 3cm	(1⅛in)

LID: START WITH A SQUARE, COLOURED SIDE UP AND COMPLETE STEPS 1 TO 8 OF THE MASU BOX (SEE PAGES 14–16).

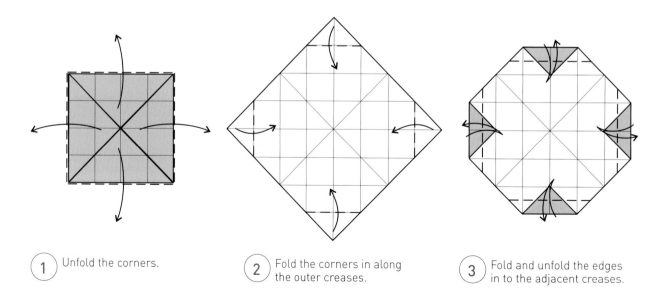

1. Unfold the corners.

2. Fold the corners in along the outer creases.

3. Fold and unfold the edges in to the adjacent creases.

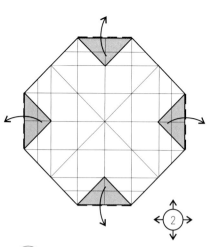

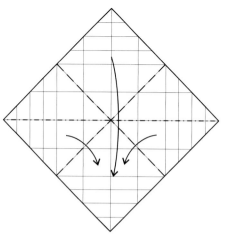

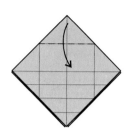

4 Unfold the corners.

5 Fold the corners in and the upper section down to make a preliminary base.

6 Fold the upper corner over along the adjacent crease.

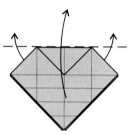

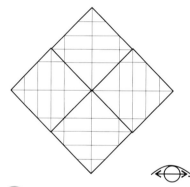

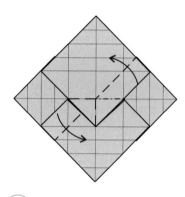

7 Open the model up by folding up the upper layer along the upper folded edge. The middle points should open up and squash flat.

8 Turn the model over, left to right.

9 Fold the two sides over to give the model a rotational symmetry. This will cause the middle section to stand up.

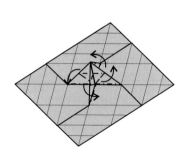

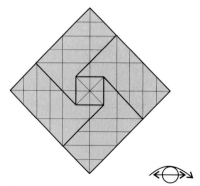

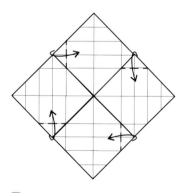

10 Twist the middle section and squash it flat.

11 Turn the model over, left to right.

12 Fold over the triangular tips of the four sections.

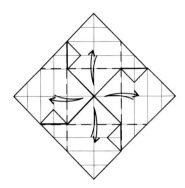

13 Fold and unfold along the creases nearest to the middle on all four sides.

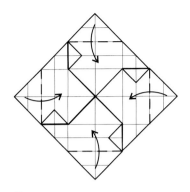

14 Fold the four corners in.

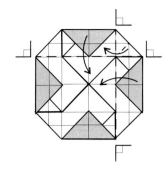

15 Fold two sides in to be perpendicular to the base. At the same time, reverse fold in the corner between the folded edges.

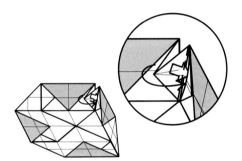

16 Fold the corner over and tuck it into the adjacent pocket.

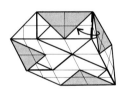

17 Fold the corner back to lie flush with the adjacent side.

(15–17) x 3

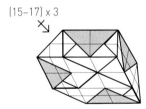

18 Repeat steps 15 to 17 on the other three corners.

19 Fold the edge over along the middle to narrow the rim of the lid.

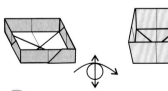

20 Turn the lid upside down. Make a Masu box (see page 14), from a similar-sized square, as a base.

21 Place the lid on the base to complete the box.

Nile
**

The triangular Nile box is based around an equilateral triangle shape that emerges from folding a square into seven sections. The outer two sections fold over to become the folded edge of the box. The Nile box is also used as a lid for some of the triangular modular boxes.

LID   18 X 18CM (7 X 7IN)

x1

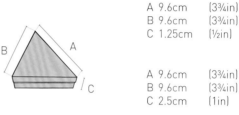

A 9.6cm   (3¾in)
B 9.6cm   (3¾in)
C 1.25cm (½in)

BASE   17 X 17CM (6⅔ X 6⅔IN)

x1

A 9.6cm   (3¾in)
B 9.6cm   (3¾in)
C 2.5cm   (1in)

The Nile box is made from two squares. The base should be made from a slightly smaller square than that of the lid. The length and width of the base should be about 1cm/½in less than the lid.

LID AND BASE: START WITH A SQUARE, COLOURED SIDE UP.

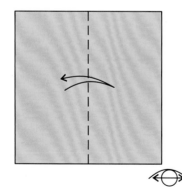

1 Fold and unfold the square in half lengthwise. Then turn the model over, left to right.

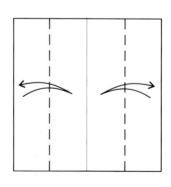

2 Fold the side edges in to touch the middle crease, and unfold.

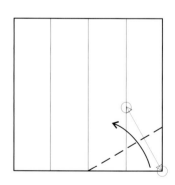

3 Fold the lower corner up to touch the vertical crease. The fold should start from the middle crease.

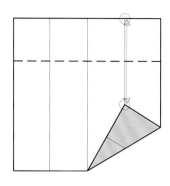

(4) Fold the upper edge down to touch the folded corner.

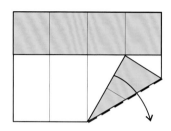

(5) Unfold the corner.

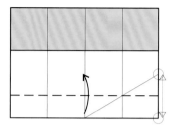

(6) Fold the lower section up. The right corner should touch the point where the crease touches the edge.

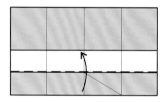

(7) Fold the lower section up again.

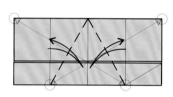

(8) Fold and unfold the upper corners over to touch the lower folded edge, as shown.

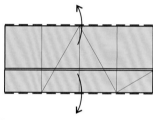

(9) Fold the upper and lower edges back out, keeping the first fold in the lower section.

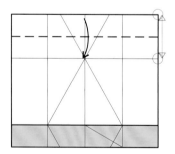

(10) Fold the upper section down.

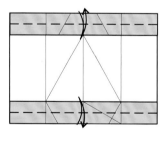

(11) [This step is for the lid and not required for the base.] Fold and unfold the edges.

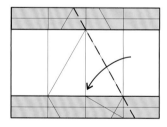

(12) Fold one side over along the crease made previously.

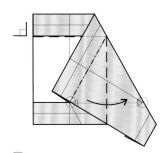

(13) Fold the section back again. This will cause the outer edges to stand perpendicular to the base.

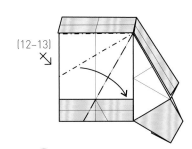

[12–13]

(14) Fold the other side in, repeating steps 12 to 13.

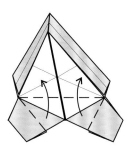

(15) Fold the lower section up to be perpendicular to the base. Open the front layer and align the edges with the adjacent sides.

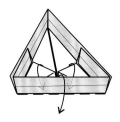

(16) Fold the section back again.

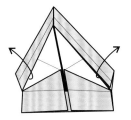

(17) Fold up the inner layer of the sides on both sides.

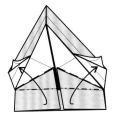

(18) Refold the lower section up. Tuck edges into sides.

(19) The base is complete.

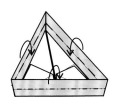

(20) Make a lid from a second square and fold the edges in along the creases made in step 11.

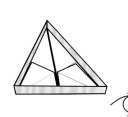

(21) Turn the lid over, top to bottom.

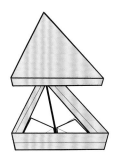

(22) Place the lid onto the triangular base.

(23) Complete.

Madeira

***

The Madeira box is a series of models that make box shapes with five, six or eight sides. The upper section of the box is closed by folding the edges in at an angle relevant to the shape of the box. The overlap of the twist forms a flower shape as decoration for the lid.

Madeira - 8-sided

LID   18 X 9CM (7 X 3½IN)   x1

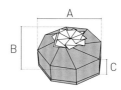

A 5cm   (2in)
B 5cm   (2in)
C 1.5cm (⅗in)

BASE 17 X 9CM (6⅔ X 3½IN)   x1

OCTAGONAL VERSION (8-SIDED BOX)
THIS MODEL IS MADE FROM TWO 2 X 1 RECTANGLES.
FOR THE LID, START WITH A 2 X 1 RECTANGLE, COLOURED SIDE UP

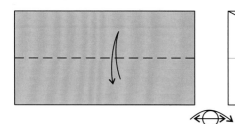

(1) Fold and unfold the rectangle in half lengthwise. Then turn the paper over, left to right.

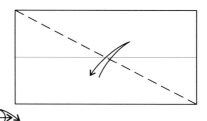

(2) Fold and unfold diagonally between the opposite corners of the rectangle.

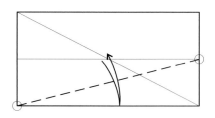

(3) Fold and unfold diagonally between the corner and the point where the middle crease touches the edge.

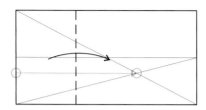

4 Fold the left side in to touch the intersection of the two diagonal creases.

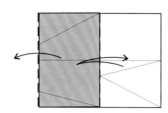

5 Fold the opposite side over the folded edge, then unfold both sides.

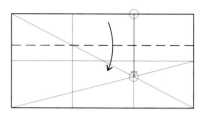

6 Fold the upper section down so the edge touches the intersection of the creases.

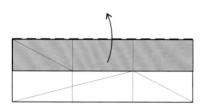

7 Unfold the upper section.

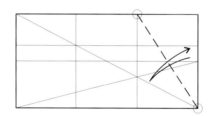

8 Fold and unfold diagonally between the first vertical crease and the lower corner.

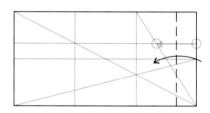

9 Fold the right side in to meet the intersection of the creases.

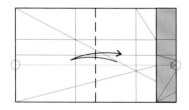

10 Fold and unfold the opposite side to the folded edge.

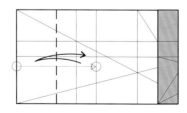

11 Fold the outer edge in to the crease and unfold.

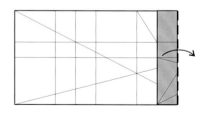

12 Unfold the outer section.

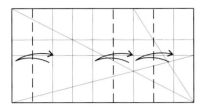

13　Fold and unfold midway between the vertical creases to divide the rectangle into nine sections.

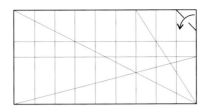

14　Fold the upper right corner in to align the upper edge with the first vertical crease.

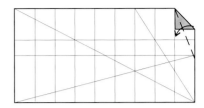

15　Fold the edge over again to align the folded edge with the vertical crease.

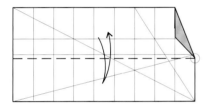

16　Fold and unfold the lower section up along a horizontal crease aligned with the lower corner of the folded section.

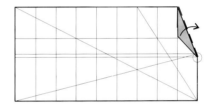

17　Unfold the folded section.

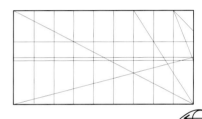

18　Turn the model over, left to right.

19　Fold and unfold a series of diagonal folds in the upper section along the middle of the rectangles formed by the vertical folds and the horizontal crease made previously.

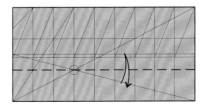

20　Fold and unfold the lower section along a horizontal crease aligned with the intersection of the creases. Make sure the edges are aligned.

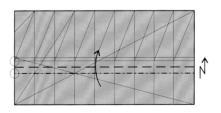

21　Fold the lower section up and down again to create a zigzag fold that aligns with the lower end of the diagonal folds made previously.

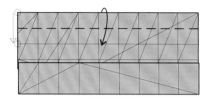

(22) Fold the upper edge over to the point where the first horizontal crease touches the outer edges.

(23) Refold and unfold the diagonal folds in the upper section.

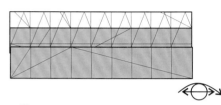

(24) Turn the model over, left to right.

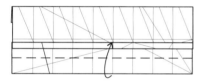

(25) Fold the lower edge up to the folded edge above.

(26) Fold and unfold the vertical creases.

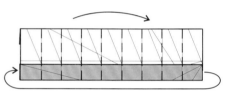

(27) Curve the model round and align the edges of the opposite sides.

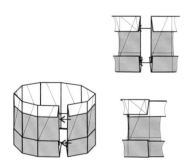

(28) Insert one edge of the model into the other. The detail shows how the layers should be inserted to lock them together.

(29) Fold and twist the upper section down, anticlockwise, as shown, to lock together.

(30) Lid complete.

MADEIRA - BASE

THE BASE IS MADE FROM A 2 X 1 RECTANGLE THAT IS SLIGHTLY SMALLER THAN THE LID.
THE STARTING RECTANGLE SHOULD BE ABOUT 1CM (½IN) NARROWER THAN THE LID.

START WITH A 2 X 1 RECTANGLE, COLOURED SIDE UP.

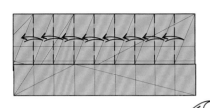

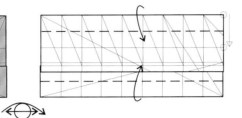

31. Follow the instructions to make the lid up to and including step 21. Then refold the vertical creases. Turn the model over, left to right.

32. For the upper section, fold the edge down to the crease. For the lower section, fold the edge in to the upper folded edge.

33. Refold and unfold the diagonal folds as shown.

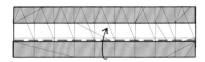

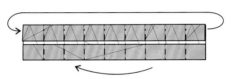

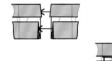

34. Fold the lower section up.

35. Curve the model round and tuck one end into the other. The back of the image should be inside.

36. Insert one end into the other, slotting it between the folds to lock them together.

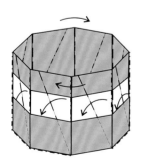

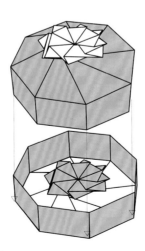

37. Rotate the inner section clockwise and flatten. The folds should start from the lower edge to form a base.

38. Place the lid onto the base.

39. Complete.

Madeira - 6-sided

LID 18 X 9CM (7 X 3½IN) x1

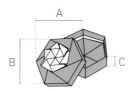

A 4cm   (1²⁄₅in)
B 4cm   (1²⁄₅in)
C 1.5cm   (³⁄₅in)

BASE 17 X 9CM (6²⁄₃ X 3½IN) x1

THE METHOD FOR MAKING THE HEXAGONAL BOX IS SIMILAR TO THAT OF THE OCTAGONAL BOX (SEE PAGE 84). HOWEVER, THE PAPER USED IS DIVIDED INTO EIGHT SECTIONS, RATHER THAN NINE.

LID AND BASE: START WITH A 2 X 1 RECTANGLE, COLOURED SIDE DOWN.

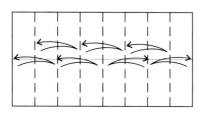

1 Fold and unfold the rectangle into eight sections (folding it in half and then between the creases).

2 Fold the lower left corner up to touch the middle crease. The fold should start from the upper left corner.

3 Unfold the corner.

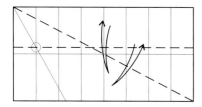

4 Fold and unfold between the opposite corners and horizontally at the intersection of the creases.

5 Fold and unfold a series of diagonal folds between the opposite corners of the upper rectangles. Then turn the model over left, to right.

6 Fold the lower section up and down again. The upper folded edge of the lower section should be aligned with the lower end of the diagonal folds.

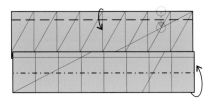

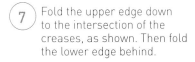

(7) Fold the upper edge down to the intersection of the creases, as shown. Then fold the lower edge behind.

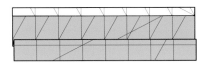

(8) Turn the model over, left to right.

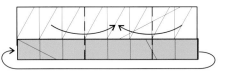

(9) Curve the model and tuck two segments of one end of the model into the other end. The final loop will be made of six sections.

(10) Open the model out to a loop.

(11) Rotate and flatten the upper section to complete the lid.

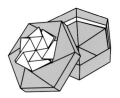

(12) Using a second rectangle repeat the base-making process from page 89 to complete the project.

Madeira - 5-sided

LID 18 X 9CM (7 X 3½IN)

    x1

A 5.75cm   (2¼in)
B 1.5cm   (⅜in)
C 4.5cm   (1⁶/₇in)

BASE 17 X 9CM (6⅔ X 3½IN)

    x1

THE METHOD FOR MAKING THE PENTAGONAL MADEIRA BOX IS SIMILAR TO THE MADEIRA 6 AND 8 (SEE PAGES 84 AND 90), HOWEVER THE PAPER USED IS DIVIDED INTO SIX SECTIONS.

START WITH A 2 X 1 RECTANGLE, COLOURED SIDE DOWN, AND COMPLETE STEPS 1 TO 5 OF THE OCTAGONAL MADEIRA (PAGES 84–6).

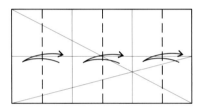

1 Fold and unfold vertically between the creases to divide the rectangle into six sections.

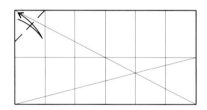

2 Fold and unfold the upper left corner in to align the upper edge with the adjacent vertical crease.

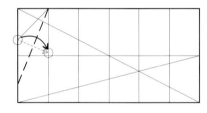

3 Fold the corner in to align the diagonal crease with the adjacent vertical crease.

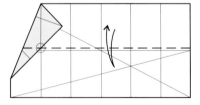

4 Fold and unfold the lower section. The horizontal crease should touch the point where the vertical crease meets the edge of the folded corner.

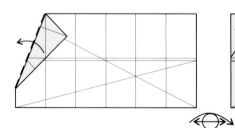

5 Unfold the corner. Then turn the model over, left to right.

6 Fold and unfold a series of diagonal folds between the upper and lower corners of the upper rectangles.

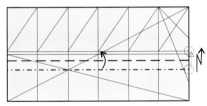

(7) Fold the lower section up and down again, making a zigzag fold. The folded edge should touch the lower end of the diagonal creases.

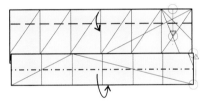

(8) Fold the upper edge down to the intersection of the creases, as shown. Then fold the lower edge behind.

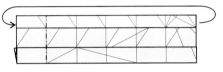

(9) Curve the model round and insert one end of the model into the other. This will make a loop with five segments.

(10) Twist the upper section anticlockwise and flatten. Make the base in a similar way and following the flattening process on page 89.

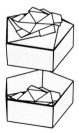

(11) Place the lid onto the base.

(12) Complete.

MODULAR
BOXES

Oolong

*

Each unit of the Oolong box forms a side of the box as a two-by-one rectangle. the project combines four units in complementary colours. The upper and lower sections have corners that weave together to lock the box.

18 X 18CM (7 X 7IN)   x4

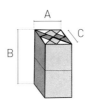

A 4.5cm   (1¾in)
B 9cm   (3½in)
C 4.5cm   (1¾in)

FOR EACH OF THE FOUR UNITS START WITH A SQUARE, COLOURED SIDE UP.

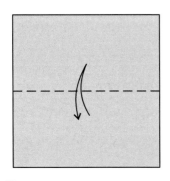

1   Fold and unfold the square in half lengthwise.

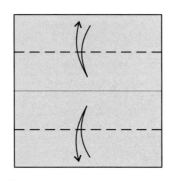

2   Fold the edges to touch the middle crease, and unfold.

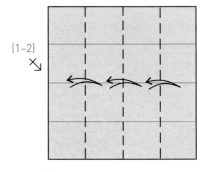

3   Repeat the process on the other axes to divide the paper into 16 sections.

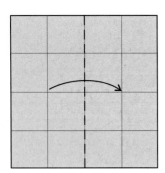

4   Fold one side over along the middle.

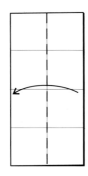

5   Fold the edge of the upper layer back over.

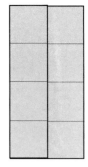

6   Turn the model over, left to right.

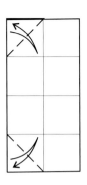

7 Fold and unfold the outer corners.

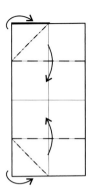

8 Fold the upper layer of the edges in, then open and squash the corners.

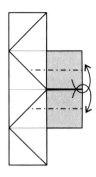

9 Fold the edges inside on the upper and lower sections.

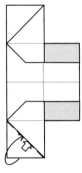

10 Fold the lower corner up and beneath the layer above.

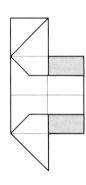

11 Turn the model over, left to right.

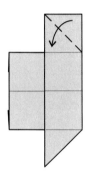

12 Fold the upper corner down.

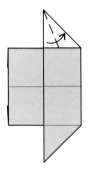

13 Fold the corner back to the folded edge.

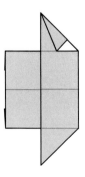

14 Module complete. Make four modules in complementary colours to complete the box. Turn the units over.

+1

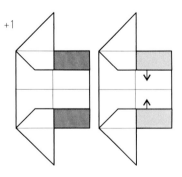

15 Joining two units. Fold out the inner layers in one of the units.

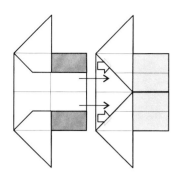
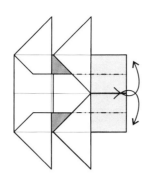
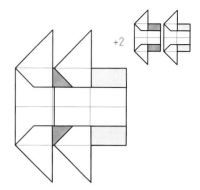

(16) Insert one module inside another.

(17) Fold the layers back in and around the edges of the other module.

(18) Add two more units using the method explained in steps 15 to 17.

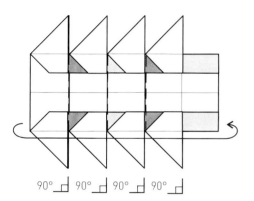

90° 90° 90° 90°

(19) Fold the modules to be perpendicular to each other and insert the modules at either end into each other.

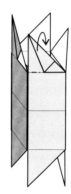

(20) Fold one corner in.

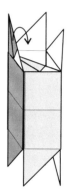

(21) Fold the adjacent corner in on top of the previously folded corner.

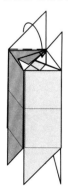

(22) Fold the next corner in.

(23) Fold the final corner in and tuck the tip in beneath the first folded corner.

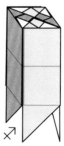

(20–23)

(24) Repeat the folds on the base (steps 20–23).

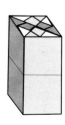

(25) Complete.

Jasmine

*

Modular boxes are made from similar units. This allows experimentation with different colours, patterns and textures. The Jasmine uses four same-sized squares for the top and the base.

18 X 18CM (7 X 7IN)

x4 x2

A	9cm	(3½in)
B	3.5cm	(1⅖in)
C	9cm	(3½in)

LID: EACH OF THE FOUR UNITS START WITH A SQUARE, COLOURED SIDE DOWN.

1 Fold and unfold the square in half lengthwise. Then turn the model over, left to right.

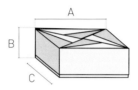

2 Fold and unfold one side diagonally along the middle.

3 Fold the lower edge to the middle, and unfold. Then turn the model over, left to right.

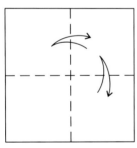

4 Fold and unfold between the creases made previously. Then turn the model over, left to right.

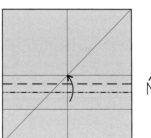

5 Fold the lower section up and down again between the creases, making a zigzag fold.

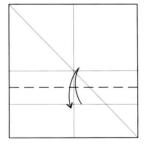

6 Turn the model over, left to right.

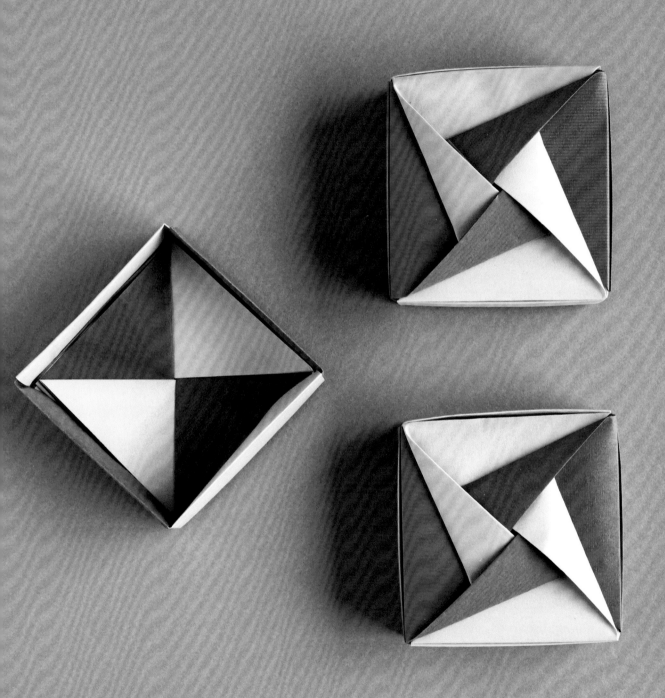

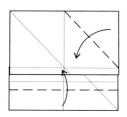

(7) Fold the upper right corner down to touch the lower crease. Fold the lower edge up to the crease above.

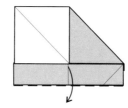

(8) Unfold the lower edge. Then make three more units in complementary colours.

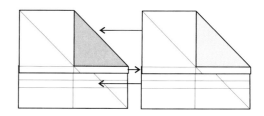

(9) Connect two parts by sliding the pleats together as shown.

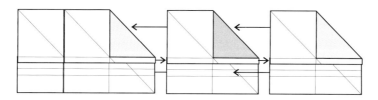

(10) Make and join two more units to have four connected sections.

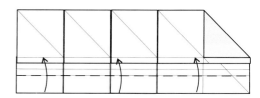

(11) Fold the lower edge up again to lock the four units together.

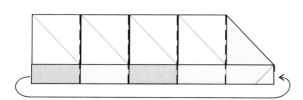

(12) Fold the model round and connect the two end units to link all four units together.

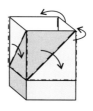

(13) Twist the upper section together and flatten.

Top view.

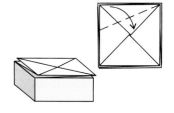

(14) The following steps show the upper view of the model. Fold one corner in to the middle.

(15) Fold the adjacent corner over the top of the folded corner.

(16) Fold the next corner in and over.

(17) Fold the corner over again and tuck the upper corner inside.

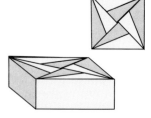

(18) Lid complete.

BASE

THE BASE IS MADE FROM FOUR SIMILARLY-SIZED SQUARES. FOR EACH UNIT START WITH STEPS 1 TO 8 OF THE LID (SEE PAGES 100–102).

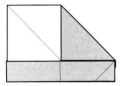 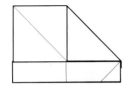

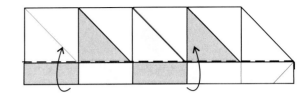

(19) Link four units together by inserting the lower sections into each other.

(20) Fold the lower edge up along all four linked units.

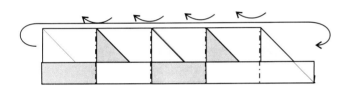

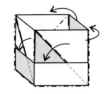

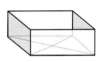

(21) Fold the end units behind and link the two ends together. The folded band should be on the outside.

(22) Rotate and squash the inner section.

(23) Base complete.

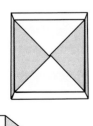

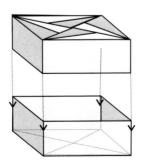

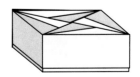

(24) Now make a lid by following a similar process.

(25) Rotate and align the base and the lid, then place the lid onto the base.

(26) Complete.

Sencha
**

The Sencha is a neat triangular box made from three similarly-sized units. The pattern on the final model uses both sides of the paper. For a snug-fitting lid, made by following the instructions for a Nile box (see page 80), use a slightly larger square than that used to make the base.

18 X 18CM (7 X 7IN)

x 3 +1

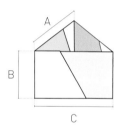

A 8cm   (3in)
B 5.4cm (2⅛in)
C 8cm   (3in)

BASE

FOR EACH OF THE THREE UNITS FORMING THE BASE START WITH A SQUARE, COLOURED SIDE UP.

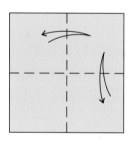

1. Fold and unfold the square in half lengthwise along both axes.

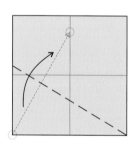

2. Fold the lower left corner up to touch the vertical middle crease as shown.

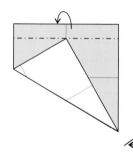

3. Fold the upper edge behind, aligned with the white folded corner. Then turn the model over, left to right.

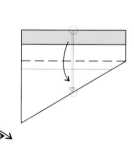

4. Fold the upper edge over.

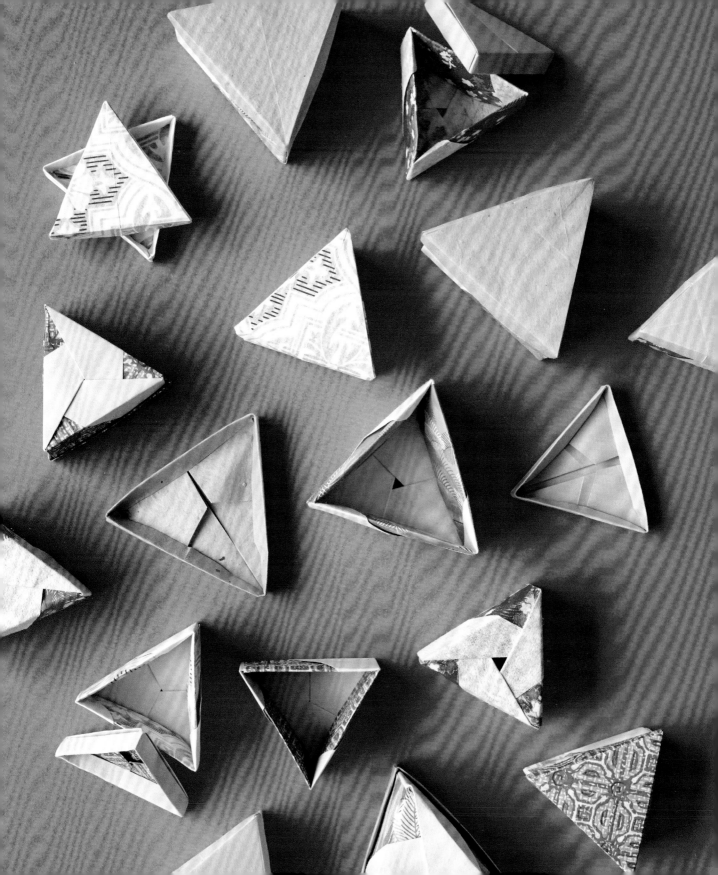

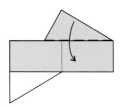

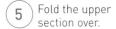

(5) Fold the upper section over.

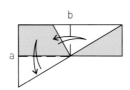

(6) Fold and unfold the lower section (a) and along the middle (b).

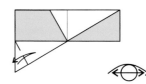

(7) Fold the corner over. The fold should be perpendicular to the edge. Then turn the model over, left to right.

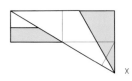

(8) Make three units in complementary colours.

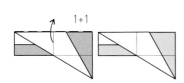

(9) To join two units together, fold the upper layer of one up.

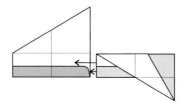

(10) Insert one unit into another.

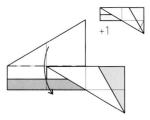

(11) Fold down the upper section and add a third unit in the same way.

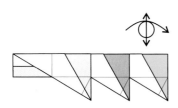

(12) Turn the model over, top to bottom.

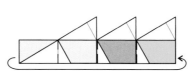

(13) Insert one end into the other to join the line of units together.

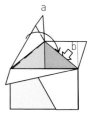

(14) Fold the corner (a) over to be perpendicular to the edge and insert the corner (a) into the pocket (b).

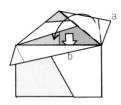

(15) Fold the next corner over and insert corner (a) into pocket (b).

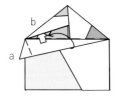

(16) Repeat the corner-folding process and fold corner (a) into the hidden folded edge(b). This might be a bit tricky.

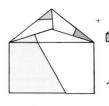

(17) Turn model over, top to bottom. Make a lid (see Nile box, page 80).

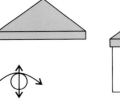

(18) Complete.

Assam

✳✳

The Assam box is similar to the Sencha. However, the box is shorter and also has an upper section. The final model is coloured with patterns from the front and back of the paper. Use a Nile box (see page 80) as a lid. The square used for the lid should be slightly larger than the squares used to make the base.

18 X 18CM (7 X 7IN)

x 3 + 1

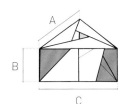

A 8.5cm   (3⅓in)
B 4cm   (1⅔in)
C 8.5cm   (3⅓in)

BASE

FOR EACH OF THE THREE UNITS FORMING THE BASE START WITH A SQUARE, COLOURED SIDE UP.

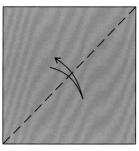

1. Fold and unfold the square in half diagonally. Then turn the model over, left to right.

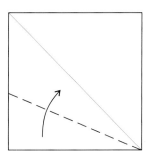

2. Fold the lower edge up to touch the crease made previously.

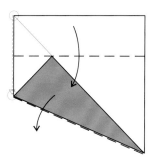

3. Fold the upper section over, aligned with the corner of the folded section. Then unfold the lower section.

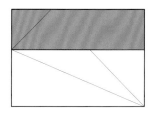

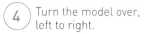

4. Turn the model over, left to right.

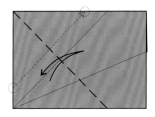

5. Fold and unfold the corner up to the folded edge.

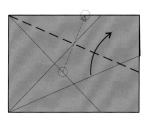

6. Fold the lower section up to align the crease with the folded edge.

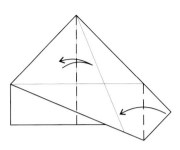

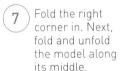

7 Fold the right corner in. Next, fold and unfold the model along its middle.

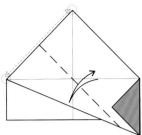

8 Fold and unfold between the corners, making a crease parallel with the outer edge.

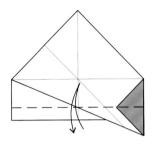

9 Fold and unfold the lower section at the point where the middle crease touches the folded edge.

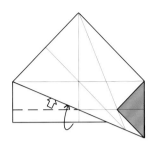

10 Fold the lower layer behind, along the crease made previously.

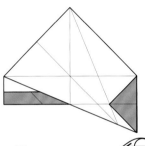

11 Turn the model over, left to right.

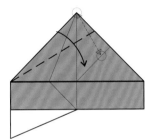

12 Fold the upper corner down to touch the adjacent diagonal crease.

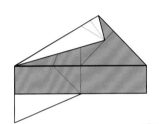

13 Turn the model over, left to right.

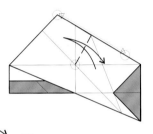

14 Fold and unfold perpendicular to the edge. The crease should start from the point where the creases intersect.

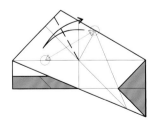

15 Fold and unfold diagonally between the creases indicated.

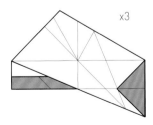

x3

16 Module complete. Make three in total, in complementary colours.

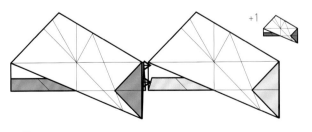

+1

17 Insert one module inside the other. The rear section of one module should fit inside the folded edges of the other, locking them together. Then add a third module in the same way.

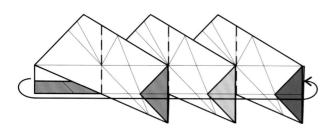

(18) Connect the ends of outer modules to make a triangular shape.

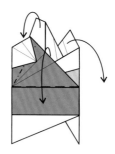

(19) Fold out the three upper points to be perpendicular to the sides. The adjacent paper will fold in and close the base.

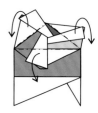

(20) Fold the sides down to be flush with the lower faces.

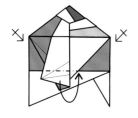

(21) Fold the end of the folded flap behind and into the pocket behind. Repeat on all sides.

(22) Turn the model over, top to bottom.

(23) Fold all of the sides in. They will overlap. The next step will show a view of the top.

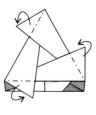

(24) Fold the corners down to be flush with the lower faces.

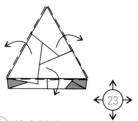

(25) Unfold the upper folded flaps.

(26) Fold the upper sections in again and tuck the wider ends beneath the narrower ends.

(27) Add a lid by making a Nile box (see page 80) using a slightly larger square.

(28) Complete.

Darjeeling
✳✳

The Darjeeling is a multi-piece variation of the Madeira box (see page 84). The modular approach enables you to create boxes in different colours and patterns by combining different papers. The models here have been made using complementary colours presented symmetrically. However, do experiment with other ideas.

18 X 18CM (7 X 7IN)

x4 x 2

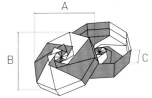

A 15.6cm (6in)
B 15.6cm (6in)
C 5.1cm   (2in)

THE LID AND THE BASE ARE BOTH MADE FROM FOUR SAME-SIZED SQUARES. MAKE THE LID FIRST. FOR EACH OF THE FOUR UNITS START WITH A SQUARE, COLOURED SIDE UP.

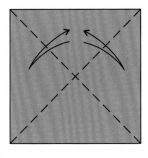

1 Fold and unfold the square in half diagonally. Then turn the paper over, left to right.

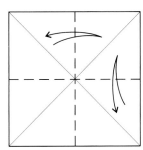

2 Fold and unfold the square in half lengthwise, along both axes.

3 Fold and unfold between the upper left corner and the middle crease.

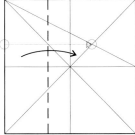

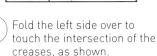

4 Fold the left side over to touch the intersection of the creases, as shown.

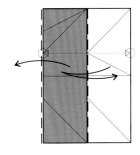

5 Fold the right side over the folded edge then unfold back to a square.

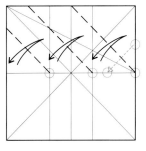

6 Make a series of 45° diagonal folds starting where the horizontal and vertical creases intersect.

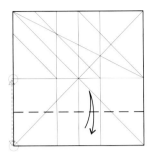

(7) Fold and unfold the lower edge up to the middle crease.

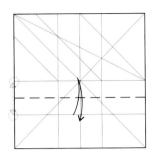

(8) Fold and unfold between the creases made previously. Then turn the model over, left to right.

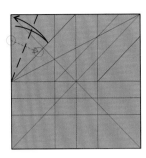

(9) Fold the upper left corner in so that the left edge touches the adjacent diagonal crease. Then unfold.

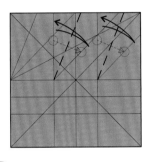

(10) Repeat the process to make diagonal folds between the vertical and diagonal creases.

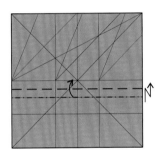

(11) Fold the lower section up and down again, for a zigzag fold. The upper folded edge should align with the middle crease.

(12) Fold the lower edge up to the folded edge, then unfold.

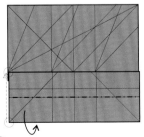

(13) Fold the edge behind along the crease made in step 12.

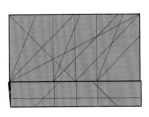

x3

(14) Unit complete. Now make three more units in complementary colours.

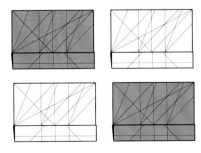

(15) Four units complete.

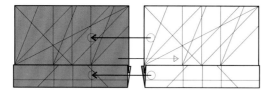

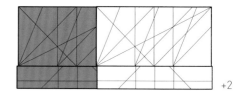

+2

16 Join two units together by slotting one in to the other. The folded layers should match up and be aligned.

17 Two units connected. Now add two more.

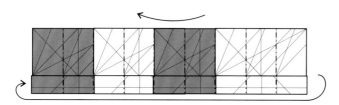

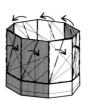

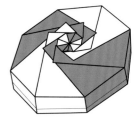

18 Curve the section around and insert one end into the other. The lower folded edge should be on the outside.

19 Twist and squash the upper section along the crease made previously.

20 Top section complete.

THE BASE IS MADE FROM FOUR UNITS. FOR EACH UNIT OF THE BASE FOLLOW STEPS 1 TO 13 OF THE LID (SEE PAGES 111 TO 113).

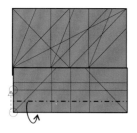

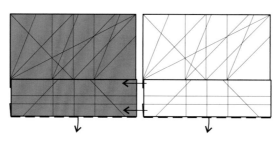

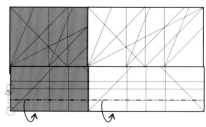

21 Fold the lower edge behind. The lower edge should touch the adjacent crease.

22 Unfold the lower edge and join two units together by inserting one unit in to another.

23 Fold the lower edge behind to lock the two sections together.

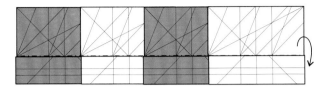

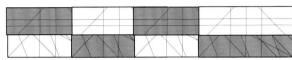

(24) Fold the upper section behind.

(25) Turn the model over, top to bottom.

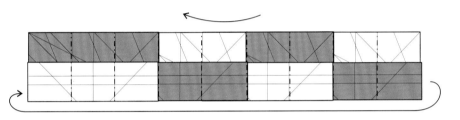

(26) Curve the model around and insert one end into the other to make an octagon shape.

(27) Twist and squash the inner section along the creases made previously.

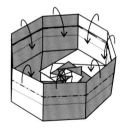

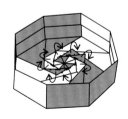

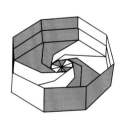

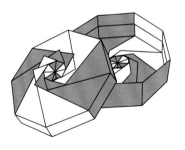

(28) Fold the edge over and into the model along the creases made previously.

(29) Fold the corners of the inner triangles on the base behind to lock the inner section.

(30) Base section complete.

(31) Put on the lid and the model is now complete.

Lapsang

***

The Lapsang weaves together six similar-sized units. Each of the units is folded from a series of equilateral triangles formed within a folded square. The box can be completed by making a hexagonal lid (the Doki, see page 66). The square used for the lid should be slightly larger than the square used for each of the base units.

18 X 18CM (7 X 7IN)

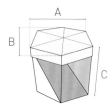

A 10cm   (4in)
B 10cm   (4in)
C 9cm   (3½in)

THE BOX IS MADE FROM SIX SIMILARLY-SIZED SQUARES.
FOR EACH OF THE SIX UNITS START WITH A SQUARE, COLOURED SIDE UP.

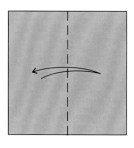

(1) Fold and unfold the square in half lengthwise. Then turn the model over, left to right.

(2) Fold the outer sides in to the middle crease, and unfold.

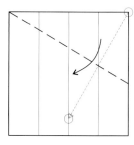

(3) Fold the upper corner down to touch the middle crease. The fold should start from the opposite corner.

(4) Fold the lower corner up, over the adjacent folded edge.

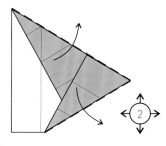

(5) Unfold back to a square.

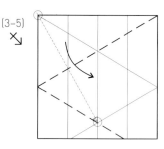

[3–5]

(6) Repeat steps 3 to 5 on the other side.

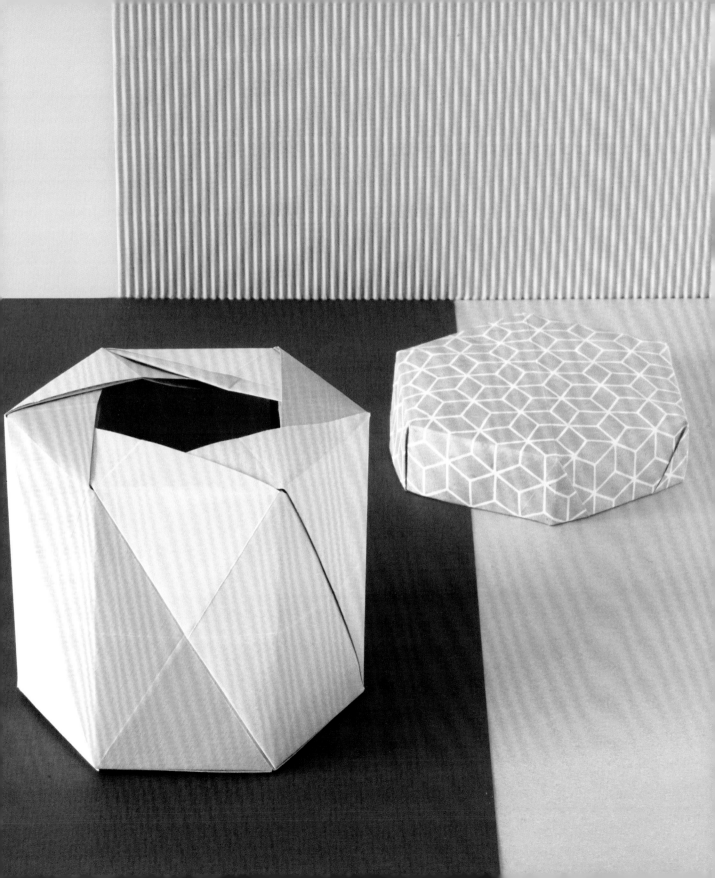

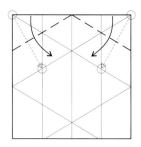

7 Fold the outer corners in to touch the intersection of the creases.

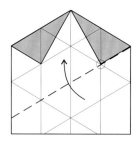

8 Fold the lower section up diagonally between the parallel diagonal folds made previously.

9 Fold the lower left corner over.

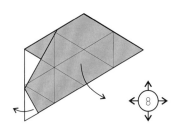

10 Unfold steps 8 and 9.

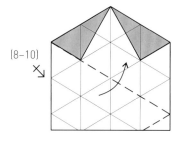

11 Repeat steps 8 to 10 on the other side.

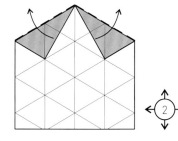

12 Unfold the upper corners back to a square (step 2).

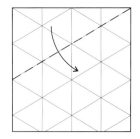

13 Fold the upper left corner down along the crease made previously.

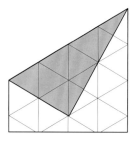

14 Turn the model over, left to right.

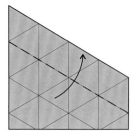

15 Fold the lower section up along the crease made previously.

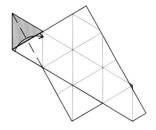

16 Fold the edge of the outer corner in, to narrow it.

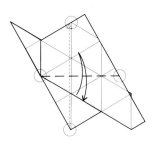

17 Fold and unfold lengthwise between the intersection of the creases.

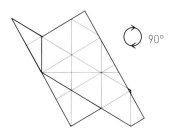

90°

18 Rotate the model by 90°.

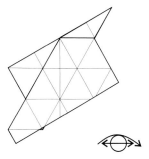

19 Turn the model over, left to right.

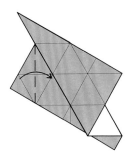

20 Fold the outer corner in.

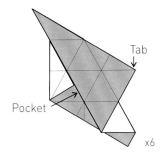

Tab

Pocket

x6

21 The module is complete. You will need six in complementary colours.

JOINING TWO MODULES

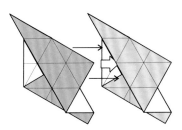

22 Insert the tab of one module into the pocket of another.

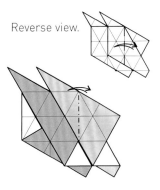

Reverse view.

23 Make a vertical crease (a mountain fold, see page 8), where the modules join.

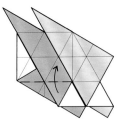

24 Fold the lower section of the inserted model up.

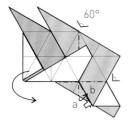

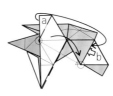

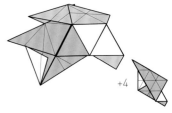

(25) Fold over the corner at (a) between the adjacent creases. Tuck the corner formed into (b) the adjacent pocket, to curve the model.

(26) Fold the section over and fold the tip (a) over and tuck it into the pocket (b).

(27) Add four more units and join them together using the process shown in steps 22 to 26.

(28) Rotate the model to look at the other side.

(29) Fold the upper corners in to the middle and tuck the outer points into the pockets in the rear side of the adjacent points to close the top of the model.

(30) Complete.

A hexagonal lid can be made by following the Doki instructions (see page 66). The starting square should be slightly larger (about 1cm/½in) than the six squares used to make the Lapsang box.

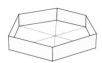

Follow the steps on pages 66 to 69.

Place the lid onto the box.

Complete.

Matcha

* * *

Matcha is made in a similar way to Lapsang. Both explore the tessellation of equilateral triangles. Matcha is less deep, with the excess paper folding neatly into a closable upper section. The model is made from six units, so try experimenting with complementary colours and textures.

18 X 18CM (7 X 7IN)

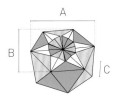

A 10.5cm   (4¹⁄₁₀in)
B 10.5cm   (4¹⁄₁₀in)
C 4.25cm   (1²⁄₃in)

MATCHA IS MADE FROM SIX SIMILARLY-SIZED UNITS. FOR EACH UNIT
START WITH A SQUARE AND COMPLETE STEPS 1 TO 13 OF LAPSANG BOX (SEE PAGES 116–18).

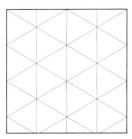

1 Rotate the model anticlockwise by 90°.

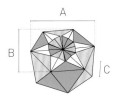
90°

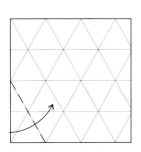

2 Fold the lower left corner in along the adjacent crease.

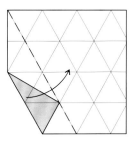

3 Fold edge over again, along the next diagonal crease.

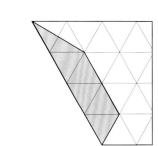

4 Turn the model over, left to right.

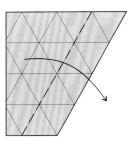

5 Fold the section over along the crease made previously.

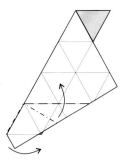

6 Fold the lower section up along the crease above so the lower section slides up.

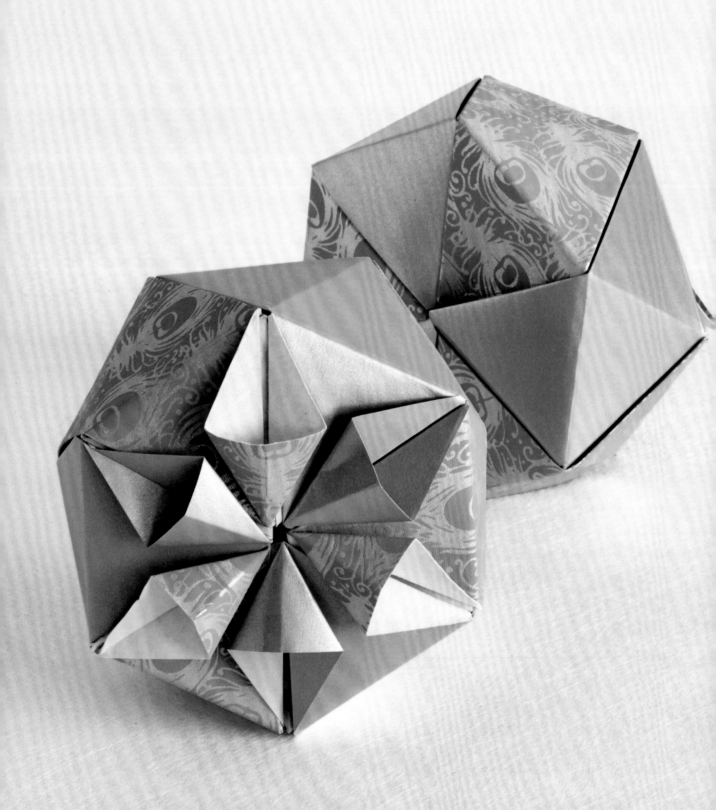

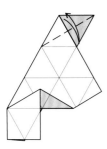

7 Fold and unfold the upper section as shown.

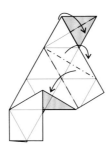

8 Fold the middle section over and refold the upper corner.

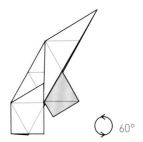

9 Rotate the model by 60°.

60°

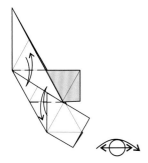

10 Fold and unfold horizontally. These creases will form the upper and lower edges of the box. Turn the model over, left to right.

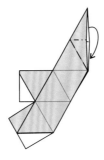

11 Fold up the upper point, separate the layers and squash the point flat.

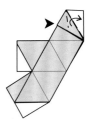

12 Fold the upper point up, separate the layers and squash the point flat.

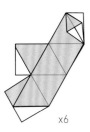

x6

13 Unit complete. Now make five more units in complementary colours.

14 Six units in total.

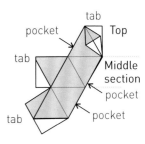

tab

pocket

Top

tab

Middle section

pocket

tab

pocket

15 The box is assembled by inserting the tabs of a unit into the pockets in adjacent units.

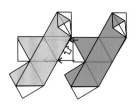

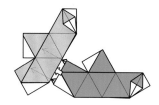

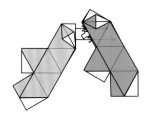

(16) The middle sections join by inserting the tab on one unit between the layers on an adjacent unit.

(17) The base is formed by inserting the tab from one unit between the layers of the adjacent unit.

(18) The upper section is joined by inserting the tab into the pocket.

JOINING UNITS

START WITH TWO UNITS AND TURN THEM BOTH OVER.

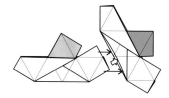

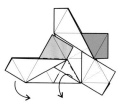

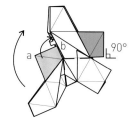

(19) Insert the tab of one unit between the layers of an adjacent unit.

(20) Make a mountain fold along the junction of the two units to align the tab of the left unit, with the edge of the right unit.

(21) Insert the tab (a) into the pocket between the layers at (b).

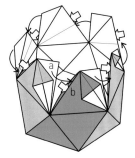

(22) Two units are joined, (steps 16 and 17). Add four more units to create a ring. The final unit should also fit into the first.

(23) Insert the tabs (a) into the pockets (b) in the adjacent units to complete the top of the box. (step 18).

(24) Complete. When all six units are connected the top should hold together.

Pekoe

✱✱

The Pekoe is a flexible module that can be used to make a four-, five- or six-sided box. For the five- and six-sided version, the model has a double-layered lid with an iris shape opening in the middle. Try experimenting with papers with different colours and textures.

18 X 18CM (7 X 7IN)

x12

A 16.2cm   (6⅓in)
B 16.2cm   (6⅓in)
C 4.8cm   (1¾in)

THE DIAGRAMS SHOW A HEXAGONAL VERSION MADE FROM 12 UNITS (6 EACH FOR THE BASE AND THE LID). MINOR VARIATIONS CAN BE MADE TO THE UNIT TO MAKE A PENTAGONAL OR SQUARE VERSION.

FOR EACH UNIT START WITH A SQUARE, COLOURED SIDE UP.

(1) Fold and unfold the square in half lengthwise. Then turn the model over, left to right.

(2) Fold the outer edges in to the middle crease. Then unfold the upper edge only.

(3) Fold and unfold the lower edge. This crease will be used when narrowing the edge of the lid.

(4) Fold and unfold the upper edge to the lower folded edge. Then turn the model over, left to right.

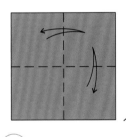

(5) Fold and unfold two diagonal folds.

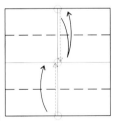

(6) Fold the upper right corner to align the outer edge with the adjacent diagonal crease.

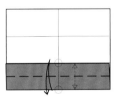

(7) Fold the corner over again along the crease made in step 5.

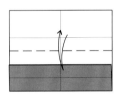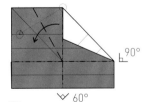

(8) Fold the upper corner down to touch the crease. The upper section will lie perpendicular to the lower section.

9 Unit complete. Now make five more for the lid and six for the base, in complementary colours.

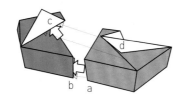

10 To link units, the edge (a) should slide into (b) and the edge (d) should slide beneath (c).

11 Two units are now connected. Now add four more.

12 Assembly complete.

13 Fold the inner edge behind to narrow the edge of the lid.

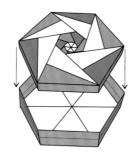

14 Make a second assembly, without narrowing the height. Then align the two parts and place the lid on the base.

15 Complete.

PENTAGONAL VERSION

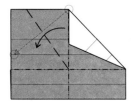

1 Complete the unit in the same way, except in step 8 fold the corner to the second crease.

2 Make four units for the lid and the base and assemble them using the method described in steps 10 to 15, above.

3 Complete.

SQUARE VERSION

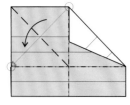

1 Complete the unit in the same way, except in step 8 fold the corner to the third crease.

2 Make four units for the lid and the base and assemble them using the method described in steps 10 to 15 above.

3 Complete.

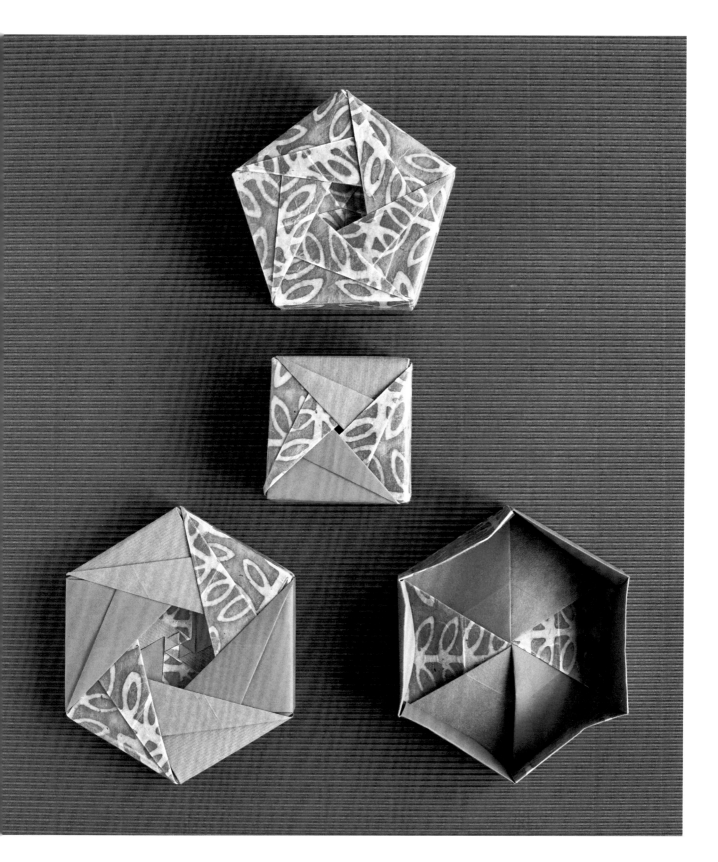

RESOURCES AND ACKNOWLEDGEMENTS

AUTHOR'S WEBSITE
Creaselightning
www.creaselightning.co.uk
Mark Bolitho's website
featuring his work.

ORIGAMI SOCIETIES
Asociación Española de
Papiroflexia (Spain)
www.pajarita.org
Spanish origami society.

British Origami Society (UK)
www.britishorigami.info
One of the oldest and most
established origami societies.

CDO (Italy)
www.origami-cdo.it
Italian origami society.

Japan Origami Academic Society
–JOAS (Japan)
Origami.gr.jp
Japanese origami association
with a good magazine on
advanced folding techniques.

MFPP (France)
www.mfpp-origami.fr
French origami society.

Nippon Origami Association
(Japan)
www.origami-noa.jp
Japanese origami society.

Origami Australia
origami.org.au
Australian origami society

Origami Deutschland
www.papierfalten.de
German origami society.

Origami USA
www.origamiusa.org
With headquarters in New York,
this society holds one of the
biggest origami conventions
of the year.

OTHER ORGANIZATIONS
Colour Tree Ltd (UK)
www.colortreelimited.co.uk
Good supplies of origami papers.

European Origami Museum
(Spain)
www.emoz.es
An origami museum in
Zaragoza, Spain.

John Gerard Paper studios
(Germany)
www.gerard-paperworks.com
Paper maker with a range of
handmade papers.

Origami Spirit (USA)
www.origamispirit.com
Origami blog and a range
of interesting projects.

Origamido Studios (USA)
www.origamido.com
A paper art studio that also
produces bespoke paper for
origami artists.

Shepherds Falkiners Fine Paper
(UK)
store.bookbinding.co.uk
UK-based supplier of fine papers.

AUTHOR'S ACKNOWLEDGEMENTS
Thanks to Marion, John, Rie, Simon, Beth, Luke, Alex, Talia, Nick, Jen, Annabelle, Jack, Ollie and Graham,
and to my friends and family for their support in my origami journey.